CRITICAL ACCLAIM FOR
THE JAN LARKIN MYSTERIES

"*The Jan Larkin Mysteries* combines the depth of classic noir with the intrigue of contemporary police procedurals to deliver three gripping novellas right up to the jagged coast of the Florida Gulf. With this latest offering, Stephen Burdick is proving his voice among the ranks of Sunshine Noir authors."
—Steph Post, author of *Lightwood*

CRITICAL ACCLAIM FOR BOOKS
BY STEPHEN BURDICK

"An authentic police voice. It's like going on a ride-along."
—Colin Campbell, author of the
Jim Grant Thrillers (for *The Gray Detective*)

"For fans of TV crime shows, Stephen Burdick's *Yesterday Rising* is one part *Bones*, one part *Cold Case Files*, and one part *Criminal Minds*."
—Tim O'Mara, author of the Raymond Donne series

"With *Yesterday Rising*, Stephen Burdick delivers a riveting read full of colorful characters."
—Joel W. Barrows, author of the Deep Cover thriller series

"*Yesterday Rising* is an engaging blend of murder, beautiful Florida settings, well-drawn characters, and challenging whodunits."
—Debra H. Goldstein, author of the Sarah Blair mystery series

THE
JAN LARKIN MYSTERIES
VOLUME 1

BOOKS BY STEPHEN BURDICK

Deemer's Inlet
The Gray Detective: Three Crime Novellas
Yesterday Rising: Three Crime Novellas
The Jan Larkin Mysteries Volume 1: Three Crime Novellas

STEPHEN BURDICK

THE
JAN LARKIN MYSTERIES
VOLUME 1

Three Crime Novellas

DOWN&OUT
BOOKS

Down & Out Books
3959 Van Dyke Road, Suite 265
Lutz, FL 33558
DownAndOutBooks.com

The characters and events in this book are fictitious. Any similarity to real persons, living or dead, is coincidental and not intended by the author.

Cover design by Dan Trudeau

ISBN: 1-64396-353-8
ISBN-13: 978-1-64396-353-2

For Claire

TABLE OF CONTENTS

ECHOES OF JANIE

PROLOGUE

If anyone had the right and the opportunity to be happy with their life, it was Janie Ballantine. Born to David and Darlene Ballantine, Janie was showered with all the possessions and creature comforts two successful lawyers could provide an only child. She had a fairy tale life. Her father was handsome, her mother beautiful, and both were intelligent and hopelessly in love with one another. Above all else, they were fiercely devoted to decency, morality, and their daughter.

In the early stages of life, Janie's charisma attracted other children who seemed to delight in her company. The few who reviled her most assumed to be consumed with envy, their misconceptions dismissed by others.

Blossoming into adulthood, Janie was blessed with a combination of her parents' physical attributes. Standing five feet eight inches tall with a well-toned figure, she possessed the commanding presence of her father. Stunning best described her beautiful face, highlighted by smooth, bronzed skin she inherited from her mother. Raven hair complemented her sapphire eyes. The only flaw on her entire body was a small, butterfly-shaped pigment beneath her left pupil. Barely noticeable at first glance, the imperfection created an air of mystery. And when she chose to speak, a clear sultry voice highlighted her skill in the art of conversation. Those fortunate enough to be deemed her friends appreciated her uniqueness.

No obstructions, pitfalls, or harbingers of evil blocked Janie's path in life. Which was why her being found dead next to the waters of the Gulf of Mexico early one spring morning struck those who loved her as unimaginable.

CHAPTER 1

Homicide Detective Jan Larkin reached for the phone lying on the table lamp next to her bed. She had been dreaming she was leaning against a pine tree, gazing upon the natural beauty of the Great Smokey Mountains outside Gatlinburg, Tennessee. Feeling robbed of the solitude she craved, she struggled to snatch the phone up before the fourth ring triggered the voicemail.

"Jan, it's Seeward."

"Yeah?" She attempted to clear the gravel from her throat, the dream still vivid in her mind.

"I'm at the Sea Castle condos in Madeira Beach." Her partner, Seeward Sinclair, sounded tentative and uneasy.

"Good for you."

"You've got to get out here ASAP."

"Christ, Seeward, it's my day off. Can't you handle it?"

"I know, Jan, and I wouldn't have bothered you except... Look, you really need to come out here."

Still, she wasn't happy about the call. "Who is it this time? A drunk fisherman fall off a boat?"

"It's Janie Ballantine."

Ordinarily, a victim's name meant little to a detective with Jan's experience. Being dulled to the news a person was dead was one of the unfortunate side effects resulting from her job. This name, though, slapped her awake.

"Janie Ballantine? As in District Attorney David Ballantine's daughter?"

"I'm afraid so. Forensics is on the way, but you've got to get out here fast. I just got word the tide will be coming in soon, and I don't want to move her before you check her out."

"I'll get there as quick as I can. You may have to do it if I get stuck in traffic."

"Just hurry, Jan...please."

"All right, I'm moving."

Jan groaned as she tossed her phone onto the bed. Seeward's reluctance to take charge of a crime scene was unusual, but no real cause for concern. He was a veteran with ten years of experience in Homicide for the Pinellas County Sheriff's Office, two years less than her, and more than capable of handling any situation. Something out of the ordinary must have happened for him to exhibit such unorthodox behavior.

Yawning, she swung her feet to the floor and stood. She stumbled after taking a step, catching herself before falling over the discarded pile of clothes. "Dammit! Someday I've got to get this place organized."

But she knew she wouldn't. Her hours on the job were long, and fatigue took control of her body the minute she set foot in the living room every night. Personal time had become a short-lived luxury, and sometimes it was non-existent. Her years as a rookie patrol officer had been a valuable learning experience in her climb up the departmental ladder. She never thought twice about the amount of time the job required. When she opted to become a detective, the hours necessary to solve a case increased. She took pride in being one of the best detectives in the department, but lately had begun to wonder if the job was worth the sacrifice.

Trudging to the bathroom, careful to watch for other objects strewn about the floor, she threw some water on her face. Gazing into the mirror above the sink, she studied the dark circles under her eyes. Her caramel-brown hair was mid-length and unfashionably tousled. Not unusual since she had never gotten the hang of styling her hair. "I look like I'm hungover," she mumbled. "I've got to take some time off."

She was once a vibrant teenager who was never concerned with her appearance. Her clothes were a perfect fit, her five-foot-eight-inch-body projected the beginning of the woman she was to become. Lack of energy was never a problem at the start of each day. She gave no thought to the future Jan Larkin. Now, at age forty-eight, she was not impressed with the woman she saw in the mirror. "Ugh," she said and threw more water on her face.

In the middle of dressing, her ex-husband's face slipped into her mind. Once again, Ken had come back to haunt her. Lines of age and time never appeared on his resilient, handsome face, magnified by tight blond curls and vibrant blue eyes. He had adored her smooth complexion and sparkling brown eyes and was always quick with a compliment. What would he say if he saw her now?

Jan sighed as she clipped her holster onto the waistband of her slacks. Melancholia had already started to work its way into a day with a dismal beginning.

CHAPTER 2

Arriving at the 132nd Avenue parking lot in Madeira Beach, Jan nodded to the deputy stationed at the entrance as she rolled past him. She steered her gray sedan into a smaller lot on the other side of Gulf Lane and eased into a space at the foot of the walkover. The entrance to the Sea Castle Condominiums opened a few feet away on her left.

Wasting no time mounting the artificial wooden bridge that lifted her over the sea oats, sea grapes, and other assorted scrub brush, she walked the sandy path that led to the beach. Carried by the wind, but more so by human traffic, the sand now covered the end of the walk-over, so leaving the structure presented no problem. The abbreviated trail of sugar sand worn through the sand dunes was a different story. Each sinking step she took in her rubber-soled leather oxfords posed a challenge. She felt the muscles in her calves tighten before she reached the packed-down grains at the shoreline.

Inside a cordoned-off section of beach, Seeward and Forensics Technician Judy Walker stood over the sand-encrusted body of Janie Ballantine. An ambulance crew with a stretcher waited nearby. Several deputies were holding back a small crowd of onlookers gawking like a flock of ravenous vultures over roadkill.

Jan ducked under the barricade tape to join the pair and the victim.

The young woman's raven-colored hair was splayed about her head and caked with sand.

"What do we know?" Jan asked.

Judy Walker continued to take pictures as she answered. "Female. Mid-twenties. Weight approximately one hundred and eight pounds. Trauma to the left side of the forehead and bruising around the throat. Looks like strangulation. A laceration and bruising on the back of the neck."

Jan leaned over to better see the head wound. "She was hit *and* strangled?"

"I'd swear to it in court." Walker sidled to her left and knelt down to get a better angle.

Jan shifted her eyes to the technician. "The laceration and bruising on the back of her neck are awfully thin. Do you think she might have been wearing some type of necklace?"

"It's possible. We'll know more when we get her on the table."

"Time of death?"

"I'd say five or six hours ago."

"Between three and four this morning."

Walker nodded.

"Who found her, Seeward?"

"Fellow standing by the dunes in the gray T-shirt and red shorts. He was jogging around six-thirty this morning."

"Any other witnesses?"

Her partner looked over his shoulder, scratched his head, then smoothed his dark brown hair. "No one in the crowd over there. I'll head to the condo and knock on some doors."

"Are you done here, Judy?"

Walker snapped another picture and lowered her camera. "I've got all I need. You look tired. Are you feeling all right?"

"You know the old saying. All work and no play."

"You're not the only detective in the department, Jan. Get some sleep, will you?"

Jan grinned as she glanced down and saw the tide encircle

her shoes before it ebbed. Sometimes she felt like the only homicide detective. The one who kept getting all the difficult cases. She turned to the ambulance crew. "Let's get her out of here before she gets washed away."

As the body was being loaded onto the stretcher, Jan headed back to her car to wait for her partner. The sugar sand and trek across the walkover did nothing to relieve the fatigue she felt. And she dreaded what she would have to do once she left Madeira Beach. Notifying the family of a murder victim was one of the most unpleasant responsibilities associated with their job. This time, the task would be especially distasteful.

Seeward strolled through the entrance to the condo much sooner than she'd expected. Depending upon the number of residents he'd interviewed, his early return was not a good sign.

"Any luck?" she said.

"There weren't many people home. One fellow, Fred Flannigan, saw two people headed to the beach early this morning. He was on his balcony smoking a cigar."

"Was he able to give you descriptions of them?"

"Not really, other than to say it was a man and woman."

Jan nodded.

"We heading back to the office?"

"Not yet. Take a couple of deputies with you and knock on some doors along Gulf Lane. Go a couple of blocks in either direction. Maybe someone saw something."

"Got it."

"I'm going to deliver the bad news to Janie's father."

"Are you sure you don't want me to come along?"

"No, it's better he hears it from someone he knows."

"You know him?"

"Kind of. I've been to his office several times. He's confided in me about certain goings-on."

"So what? That doesn't mean he considers you a friend."

"Seeward, I know he can be a hardass and won't budge an inch when he thinks he's right. And I've heard how he steps on defense attorneys who try to pull unethical bullshit, but this is personal. He needs to hear it from someone with whom he's relatively familiar. I don't believe he's going to get violent or anything."

"Well... okay."

"Seeward, I've seen you act this way before. Now what's bothering you?"

"Nothing. I just thought you'd like some company."

"Are you sure?" She'd been around Seeward long enough to know when something was troubling him. And denying anything was wrong was always his first response.

"Yes, Jan."

"Don't think for one minute I'm looking forward to seeing him. When you get done here, go back to the office and start a search on Janie Ballantine. See what you can uncover."

"Got it. Say, isn't Janie's mother an attorney too?"

"A corporate attorney, from what I understand. And just as smart and tenacious as her husband."

"Kind of makes you wonder about Janie, doesn't it?"

"That's what I want you to find out."

As she pulled out of the parking lot, Jan wondered what effect two highly intelligent and successful parents might have had on their only child throughout her life. What Janie might have done to wind up dead was as perplexing an enigma as how she was murdered and who had killed her. Another issue beginning to get under Jan's skin was the behavior of her partner. Getting him to divulge the source of his dilemma was like trying to put out a wildfire with a garden hose. She grinned. The two of them were hard-headed. They knew each other well.

When her gut tightened, she knew for certain it would be one of the most difficult cases they would attempt to solve.

CHAPTER 3

Jan was well aware District Attorney David Ballantine's case against local crime figure Colby Rittenhouse was not going well. She'd heard about the judge tossing out vital evidence due to a legal oversight, along with other negative scuttlebutt.

She felt an air of uneasiness hanging over Ballantine's office the moment she entered. Tension covered the faces of the few associates who emerged from the inner offices, paying little attention to her and others waiting to be received. Even the receptionist sat stiff and expressionless.

"How can I help you?" she said.

Jan held up her badge. "Detective Sergeant Jan Larkin, Pinellas County Sheriff's Office. I need to speak with Mr. Ballantine."

"Is he expecting you?"

"No."

"I'm sorry, but he is unavailable to meet with anyone today."

"Please let him know I'm here. This is urgent."

"I'm sorry, but unless Mr. Ballantine is expecting you, he is unavailable."

Jan started for the door to the inner offices. She didn't want to tell the receptionist what she had seen at the beach this morning..

"Wait!" the receptionist shouted. She punched the button to an interoffice line and adjusted her headset. "Yes, there's a

Detective Larkin here to see Mr. Ballantine. She says it's important." The receptionist rolled her eyes. "I explained that to her, but she's insistent." She punched the button. "Someone will be with you shortly."

A short, slender woman wearing an expression as taut as the blonde hair pulled into a bun at the nape of her neck emerged from the hallway. Black horn-rimmed glasses matched her business suit and pointed-toe pumps.

"Detective Larkin, I'm Delia Wentz, Mr. Ballantine's administrative assistant."

"Yes, I need to speak with Mr. Ballantine."

"I'm sorry, but this is not a good time. I'll be glad to make an appointment for you to see him in the next day or so."

"This can't wait."

"Is it a matter which could be handled by the assistant district attorney?"

"It's a personal matter. And it's very important."

Wentz paused and offered a blank stare. "Follow me, please."

The hallway held the atmosphere of the last corridor leading to an arena hosting a pride of lions. Jan's breathing became labored. Perspiration dangerously close to dripping from the pores under her arms added to her discomfort.

As they emerged into a smaller waiting room, Wentz turned to her. "Please wait here."

Jan watched the assistant approach the office door, pausing before she knocked. Upon entering, she left the door ajar. Seconds were slow in passing.

"Not now!" came a man's voice.

Wentz edged out of the office. "I'm sorry, Detective Larkin, but Mr. Ballantine is engaged in an important matter and does not wish to be disturbed."

"Believe me, Ms. Wentz, this is extremely important."

Jan started for the door.

Wentz stepped in front of her. "It had better be earth-shattering." She entered the office again, said something, then pulled open the door and gestured Jan inside.

David Ballantine looked like a man ready to hand down a death sentence as Jan neared his desk. His telephone rang, interrupting their meeting before it had begun. Ballantine picked up the receiver and waved Jan to one of the chairs in front of his paper-strewn desk. The thought of eavesdropping left her feeling awkward.

"No! No! No!" Ballantine shouted. "Look, I told you we don't have what we need to proceed in that direction. We're dead if we go back to court without more evidence. Now, if you can't find what I need, then I'll find someone who can!" He slammed down the receiver and took a moment to calm himself. "As you might have guessed, things are *not* going well. Now, what is so important for you to interrupt my day, Detective?"

Jan cleared her throat. "Mr. Ballantine, there's no easy way for me to say this, but you're daughter has been murdered."

Ballantine didn't react at first, his gray eyes remaining hard and narrowed. "What...

What did you just say?"

"She was discovered on the beach near her condo early this morning."

"I don't believe you."

Jan said nothing.

Ballentine's eyes softened and started to well up. "You're sure it's Janie?"

"Yes, sir."

The attorney turned his head and released a sharp breath. "How did it happen?"

"It's too early to tell. As we learn more, I'll pass along the information. Sir, I know this is a difficult time for you, but I really need to ask you some questions."

Ballantine paused, then nodded.

Jan shifted in her chair. "When was the last time you saw your daughter?"

"Last weekend, I believe. Yes. She and her friend stopped by the house on Sunday."

"Her friend?"

"Daniel Peck. She's been keeping company with him for quite a while."

Jan pulled a pen and notepad out of the pocket of her slacks. "Do you know his address?"

"No, I..." Ballantine looked up, as if trying to remember. "No."

"Is something wrong, sir?"

He shook his head then wiped his eyes with both hands.

"Do you know where he works?"

"He's a CPA, I believe. I don't know the name of his firm."

"Did your daughter seem upset the last time you saw her?"

"She was her usual self..." Ballantine looked away and cleared his throat. "Happy, always smiling."

"And Daniel Peck?"

"Daniel was nervous. But then he was always nervous around Darlene and me."

Jan noticed disbelief was gaining a foothold in Ballantine. "You said Daniel Peck was nervous. Any particular reason?"

"He always acted nervous when they came to see us. Neither he nor Janie ever told us why. Maybe he felt unwelcome." Ballantine sighed. "Detective, we want the best...wanted the best for our daughter."

"And Daniel Peck doesn't fit the mold?"

"Not in my eyes."

"You don't like him?"

"It's not a matter of like or dislike. He's not well established."

"I'm not following you."

"He lives in an apartment. We were hoping she'd find someone a bit more grounded and secure."

"Did your daughter ever mention being bothered by anyone?"

"Not to me or Darlene."

"Darlene is your wife?"

"Yes, and she would have told me."

"Where were you and your wife last night?"

"We were attending a fundraiser in downtown St. Pete. Tons of people were there who know us and can attest to our presence."

"Yes, sir, and you know I have to ask."

"I understand. Detective, if you don't mind, could we continue this at another time? I don't feel like answering anymore questions."

"Yes, sir, I'll be in touch." Jan got to her feet. "And we'll need you to identify the body."

Ballantine nodded and lowered his head.

"I'm very sorry for your loss," Jan said and quietly left his office.

CHAPTER 4

Jan breathed easier after returning to the office. Taking a seat at her desk, she pondered the unenviable plight of David and Darlene Ballantine. Only the most insensitive person could have delivered such a message without feeling something. As a veteran detective, she had witnessed some of the most heinous murder scenes imaginable. Why this case left her filled with an abundance of empathy for people, she didn't know was a mystery in itself. Some cases were like that. Some people were like that. Being the bearer of that kind of news was a necessary and unsatisfying part of the reality in which she lived.

She thought of her own nieces and nephews, knowing how she would feel if something horrifying were to happen to one of them. Rage would push her beyond the limits of reason. Of that, she was certain. A vengeful act was guaranteed if something were to happen to her favorite niece, Riley Jo. How such dreadful news would affect her brothers was not difficult to imagine. They were family. Their response would mirror hers and be one of revenge.

With leadership came responsibility, though, and she knew she must put aside her personal feelings. The sooner, the better. Hearing her partner pull out his chair to sit down chased the distressing thoughts from her head. "So, what did you find out about Janie Ballantine, Seeward?"

"No arrest warrants or traffic tickets, but check this out. She

17

graduated from the University of Florida with master's degrees in Arts History and Museum Studies. Pretty impressive, huh?"

"I'll say. I thought she'd have some job in a law office."

"And she's the curator at the Pinellas Fine Arts Museum."

"No kidding."

"Not bad for someone who just turned thirty."

"Guess she inherited her intelligence from her parents."

"Jan, I just got the preliminary back from the medical examiner. The blow to the head killed Janie."

"What about the bruising on her neck?"

"They said the strangulation occurred before the killer bashed her, caused by the links from a thin necklace."

"So, strangling her wasn't enough to get the job done, I guess."

"Maybe he surprised her, and she fought him off. Or maybe he was toying with her."

"How do you know the killer was a *he*?"

Seeward rolled his eyes and huffed. "Please excuse my politically incorrect assumption, Sergeant."

"And we don't have one piece of evidence."

"None so far. The tide took care of any footprints. And I don't have to tell you about sugar sand."

Jan knew all too well sugar sand, so named for its color and loosely packed granules, separated under the least bit of weight and sometimes filled in after a step was taken. To find any semblance of a defined footprint was rare, the result most often a gritty dimple.

"You mentioned some guy who lived in her condo," she said. "What was his name?"

"Fred Flannigan?" Seeward flipped through his notepad. "He said he was on his balcony between one-thirty and two o'clock in the morning smoking a cigar when he saw two people on the path between the dunes."

"Could he tell who they were?"

"Just a man and a woman, he said. About the time he was

going inside, he heard two people arguing."

"The same couple?"

"He couldn't tell. Just that it sounded like a man and a woman. He listened for a minute or so, and then the arguing stopped. The medical examiner puts the time of death at between three and five a.m."

"That's in keeping with what Judy Walker told us."

Jan and Seeward knew what the other was thinking. Spending more time together than being at home, and partnered longer than some people remained married made understanding the other's personality easier. Without one piece of evidence, and only one man's sketchy statement, their job became that much tougher.

"Oh, by the way, Janie Ballantine has a boyfriend," Seeward said.

"Yeah, I know. Daniel Peck. David Ballantine told me. He said Peck was a CPA or something."

"He works for Lengaard and Associates. He's twenty-eight and lives in the Big Bayou apartment building just off Seminole Boulevard."

Jan rose from her desk. "Let's go have a talk with Mr. CPA Daniel Peck."

"I called his office. They said he was out sick today."

The odd expression covering Seeward's face was hard for Jan to ignore as he stood up. An impish gleam was dancing in his eyes.

"You're not buying that excuse, are you?" she said.

"I'm thinking it's more a case of the brown bottle flu."

"Do I want to know how you came by such a deduction?"

"Oh, let's just say after talking to Erica for a while, she became very helpful."

"I take it Erica is an administrative assistant or a paralegal?"

"A most wise deduction, Sergeant."

"Was it a productive conversation?"

"You bet, once I turned on the old Sinclair charm."

19

This time, Jan rolled her eyes.

"Well, what can I say?"

"I know what I can say. I think I'm going to be sick."

"Oh! Did I mention Erica is an old high school friend of mine?"

Jan shook her head. "All right, smartass. Let's take a ride and see if Mr. Brown Bottle Flu is recuperating at home."

"Might as well. It's too wet to plow."

As she neared him, Jan took a hold of his arm. "I know I'll probably regret this, but what, exactly, does *that* mean?"

"All we know for certain is he is her boyfriend, right?"

Jan stared at him.

"So we might as well go talk to him to learn more. It's an old saying. You know, like 'might as well, we can't dance.' Or 'might as well, there's no rain on the rhubarb.'"

Jan shook her head again. "How did I ever manage to get stuck with you?"

Seeward burst into laughter as they left the Homicide office.

CHAPTER 5

The ride to Daniel Peck's apartment was quiet. Jan and Seeward had taken many rides together, and conversations teeming with various topics was their normal routine. Silence created an uncommon void between them this time. But she was pondering the troublesome lack of evidence and preparing the list of questions she was about to ask the unsuspecting boyfriend of Janie Ballantine. The tremendous amount of pressure soon to be put on them by their superiors also weighed heavily upon her..

The accountant's unpretentious residence lay two blocks west of Seminole Boulevard in the 6400 block. Seeward parked their gray sedan two spaces down from Peck's apartment, then he and Jan wasted little time in getting to his front door. "This place looks pretty ho-hum for an accountant's digs," he said.

"Maybe he's frugal."

"Or maybe he's just plain cheap."

As they stopped in front of Apartment #4, the door was slightly ajar. Seeward gave Jan a quick glance before he knocked. After several attempts, he turned to his partner. "I'll bet he's passed out in a chaise lounge by the swimming pool."

"This place is too small to have a pool."

"All right. On the sofa then."

"Ow! Goddammit!" cried a voice from inside.

The detectives stepped back.

A groggy, disheveled young man pulled open the door. The

21

pungent odor of liquor poured out of the room.

"Daniel Peck?" Jan asked.

Peck offered a tired grin. "Most of the time. But today, I'm not so sure."

Jan displayed her badge. "I'm Detective Sergeant Larkin of the Pinellas County Sheriff's Office. This is Detective Sinclair. Is everything okay? We heard someone scream."

"Stubbed my toe on the damn dining table."

"May we come in?"

"Uh, sure." Peck stepped back and pulled the door open. "Sorry the place is a mess. What's this all about?"

Jan led Seeward inside. Jan glanced at the small pockets of sand scattered over the forest green carpet and caught Seeward's eye. "Do you know a Jane Holten Ballantine?" she said.

"She's my girlfriend. Why?"

"Mr. Peck, your girlfriend was found murdered behind her condo in Madeira Beach this morning."

Peck's mouth fell open. He half-turned and hobbled a few steps before collapsing onto his slate gray sofa. "Oh, god! How... How did it..." He couldn't finish and buried his face in his hands.

Seeward sat in a gray chair next to the sofa. Jan sat down on the other end of the couch and narrowed her eyes.

Peck began to cry. Five minutes passed before he regained his composure and wiped his face with the back of his hand.

"Mr. Peck, when was the last time you saw Ms. Ballantine?" Jan said.

"Last night. We went to dinner and then to a club. What happened?"

"Where did you go to eat?"

"Lamson's Chop House. On Ulmerton Road."

"And the club you went to afterwards?"

"The Silver Sandpiper. I can't believe she's been murdered."

"I know this is difficult for you, but what time did you leave the club?"

"Between twelve-thirty and one o'clock this morning, I think."

"You don't know?" Seeward said.

"I'm not sure. I had a lot to drink. Janie wasn't happy about it."

"You were drunk, and you brought her back here?"

"No. No. She drove us to her condo."

"Her condo in Madeira Beach?"

"She wanted me to stay with her because I was wasted."

"Then you've stayed with her before."

Peck nodded.

Their conversation was interrupted when the muffled melody from a phone sounded. Confusion covered Peck's face until the second chorus drew his eyes to the crack between the sofa cushions. He retrieved the phone and answered.

"Yes, sir. Yes, sir, they're here right now. I know and I'm sorry. I'll explain everything later, I promise. Yes, sir." Peck laid the phone down beside him and focused on Jan. "My boss. He's already pissed because I'm missing work today, and now he wants to know why you called my office."

"We were trying to locate you," Jan said. "Okay, just so we're clear, Ms. Ballantine drove the two of you to her condo, you refused her invitation to spend the night, and then you drove home. Is that correct?"

"I'm pretty sure we had coffee first."

"Pretty sure?"

"Janie could be very persuasive."

"And after that you went home?"

"We went for a walk on the beach, I think."

Jan glanced at Seeward. "What did you do next?"

Peck lowered his eyes to the floor. "I'm not sure."

"Did you talk? Did you argue? Did you make love? What?"

"We talked...I think."

"What do you think you talked about?"

"I can't remember. I drank way too much last night."

"You said that. But you remember her driving you to her condo, asking you to spend the night, and serving you coffee. And then you think the two of you went for a walk on the beach. How long were you walking on the beach?"

Peck laid a hand on his forehead. "I'm not sure."

"When did you leave?"

"I don't know."

"How did you get home? Taxi? Uber? Did *she* drive you home?"

"I don't know! How many times do I have to tell you? I was drunk!"

"No need to yell, Mr. Peck. I know this is difficult, but we're trying to help you."

Peck hung his head. "I know. But I just can't believe Janie is dead."

"Is there anything else you can tell us about last night?"

"That's all I can remember."

"Here's my card. If you think of anything later, please call me."

The detectives and Peck rose from their seats.

"We'll see ourselves out," Jan said. "You take care of your foot."

They heard him start crying again as they walked out of his apartment. When they reached their car, Seeward paused by the driver's side door.

"Jan, he admitted he was with her on the beach."

"We both heard him."

"And the sand on his rug is the proof."

"Even though he says he was drunk the entire time and doesn't remember half of what they did."

"Are you good with his story?"

"I think he's either telling the truth, or he's a really good liar. He could have killed her before he drunk himself into a stupor. Either way, let's play it safe and get a search warrant."

Jan knew one thing for certain. With no clues, and a sketchy witness at Janie Ballantine's condo, the only lead they had was their conversation with Daniel Peck. And the sand on the floor of his apartment. She thought it odd he hadn't tried to dispose of the sand the previous night no matter what his condition. A thorough search of his place might uncover more incriminating evidence. On the downside, if they found nothing, they would have to go back to square one and go over the crime scene again. That notion did not sit well with her.

CHAPTER 6

The next day, Jan went to Janie Ballantine's home in the Sea Castle Condominiums to search it again—without her partner. Having directed Seeward to continue the research and fill out the necessary reports, she wanted to have a look for herself. Her partner didn't object, but she suspected something about this case was bothering him. She understood anything or anybody could disrupt a detective's course of investigation. Maybe Seeward had been introduced to Janie at some social gathering years ago. Or dated her long before he joined the sheriff's office. At the proper time, she would pull him aside and finagle the truth out of him.

The young woman's residence occupied half of the top floor in the ten-unit building. Her balcony provided an extensive view of the Gulf of Mexico. Uncertainty kept calling her name as Jan walked onto the balcony and gazed out over the sand dunes and the beach beyond. She looked down the side of the building and noticed, where the floor of the parking garage ended beneath the units, a crushed oyster shell ground cover extended out and angled downward with the contour of the lot. At the property line, the shell melded into a medley of sea grapes, beach dune sunflowers, and sea oats, the latter blanketing the sand dunes before giving way to the snow-white sands of the beach.

The balconies of the two top floor domiciles were equipped with metal spiral staircases leading to the roof. Two small sundecks divided by a vinyl fence offered a minimal amount of privacy for the owners. A benefit not afforded the other residents who lived in the units below.

After climbing the stairs to the sundeck, Jan sat down on a chaise lounge. The panoramic view was impressive. Definitely a major selling point when luring a perspective buyer.

From the lofty perch, Jan imagined the rainbow of colors marking the sky at the end of the day. Knowing Janie Ballantine would never enjoy another sunset, she felt a pang of sadness. The sight of a solitary figure interrupted her thoughts. It moved at a slow and even pace along the water's edge. The figure appeared to be holding a metal detector, sweeping it back and forth in perfect rhythm.

She leapt from the chair and hurried down the staircase before dashing through the condo to the hall and elevator. Close to a full sprint by the time she traversed the walkover, she slowed to a jog once she reached the path between the dunes. When she finally set foot on the beach, she discovered the person wielding the device was an elderly man.

Five feet four or five inches tall at best, his bushy white beard lay full over his acorn-brown face. Collar-length disheveled white hair protruded from under a khaki-colored cap that sported an extended green plastic bill. A style popular among many old-time anglers. With the sleeves rolled up above his elbows, his khaki shirt was unbuttoned halfway down his chest and revealed a good-sized tuft of snow-white hair. The legs of his khaki trousers bunched up mid-calf around his spindly brown legs. He'd likely been a commercial fisherman and epitomized Old Florida. The old man glanced at her as she approached, then resumed his quest.

"Excuse me, sir," Jan said.

The old man ignored her and continued to slosh along the shore.

"Sir? Sir, I'd like a word with you."

The old man huffed and yanked the earphones from his

head. "Whaddaya want?"

Jan displayed her badge. "I'm Detective Sergeant Larkin, Pinellas County Sheriff's Office. Can I ask you a few questions?"

The old man hesitated and offered a suspicious eye. "Do I gotta choice?"

"I'd appreciate it."

"Aw right."

"Do you come here every day?"

"Nope. Not *here* ever day."

"Were you here a few days ago?"

"Mebbe."

"You don't remember?"

"Coulda been."

"What's your name, sir?"

"Phillips. Morton Phillips. Some folks calls me Crabby, though."

"Crabby, huh? Then I take it you must be a crab trapper."

"Nope."

"Oh? Then why *do* folks call you Crabby?"

"What the hell's it to ya?"

Jan almost laughed out loud, but maintained her professionalism. "Do you mind if I call you Crabby?"

Again, the old man hesitated. "S'pose not."

"Okay, Crabby. If you *were* here a few days ago, did you find anything other than the usual trinkets and coins?"

Crabby didn't answer right away, and looked at her as if she were a sea creature he'd never seen before. "Nope."

"You didn't come across anything out of the ordinary? Something that might seem out of place on the beach?"

"That's what I said. Yer hearin' bad?"

Jan lowered her eyes to the sand. "No, I heard you. I was just hoping you might have found... Well, thanks anyway, Crabby."

"Whatcha huntin' fer?"

"I'm not sure."

"Is this 'bout that girl who was killed t'other day?"

Jan looked up. "Yes, it is." She thought she saw a glimmer of sympathy in the old fisherman's eyes.

"Naw. I didn't find nothin' I ain't found 'ere b'fore. Nothin' worth jawin' 'bout anyways."

"Well, thanks for your time, Crabby. It was nice to meet you."

"You, too, Cap'um."

Jan smiled. "Sergeant."

Crabby smiled back at her, displaying a mouthful of yellow-tinged teeth.

As Jan struggled through the sugar sand and mounted the incline of the walkover, she happened to look down when she grabbed hold of the railing. Part of a flat, singed piece of wood coated with grains of sand stuck out beside the support piling. She knelt down for a closer look. The object was not made of wood, nor was it singed. Jan reached into the back pocket of her slacks and pulled out an evidence bag. Sticking her hand inside the bag, she carefully picked up a small pry bar.

"I wonder if this was used to kill Janie Ballantine," she whispered.

CHAPTER 7

Two days dragged by before Jan and Seeward found themselves en route to Daniel Peck's apartment. Judge Michael Quinzi had agreed to their request for a search warrant.

"Are you surprised Judge Quinzi gave the go ahead, Jan?"

"Not really. He's a believer in probable cause. And I understand Quinzi and David Ballantine go way back."

As they entered the parking lot, Seeward was able to steer their car into a space directly in front of Apartment #4. Exiting the car, they were careful in approaching the door. Jan nodded to Seeward, and he pounded on it three times.

When the door swung open, Daniel Peck looked as haggard and rumpled as he had during their first visit.

"What's all this?" he asked.

"Daniel Peck, we have a warrant to search your apartment," Jan said. She thrust the document at him. "Please step aside."

Astounded, Peck did as she ordered and stared at the paper in his hands.

Seeward moved past him and proceeded to rummage through the closets, rooms, and other belongings in his apartment. Jan noticed the clumps of sand that still dotted the carpet.

Peck looked up from the warrant. "Wait a minute! Do you think I killed Janie? I loved her. I would never do anything to hurt her."

"Mr. Peck, please let us do our job."

Fear widened Peck's eyes. "You got to believe me. I didn't kill her. I loved her."

Jan had seen too many bodies and heard too many cries of innocence to be persuaded. A number of suspects before him had used love as an alibi, and many had turned out to be killers.

Peck shuffled to the sofa and sat down.

Twenty minutes passed.

Seeward emerged from the bedroom with a golden crucifix on the end of a broken chain dangling from his right hand. "I found this hidden in the bedroom closet." He glanced at the crucifix, then leveled accusing eyes on Peck.

"That belongs to Janie," Peck said.

"Then what was it doing in your closet?"

"She likes to hide things."

"I didn't find anything else that looked like it might belong to her."

"Why does she like to hide her things from you?" Jan said.

"She wants me to think about her when I find them, I guess. She likes to play games. I don't know."

"You don't know. So, we're back to that again."

Seeward pulled an evidence bag out of his coat pocket and dropped the crucifix inside.

"Don't get any ideas about leaving town without contacting us first, Mr. Peck," Jan said.

"We may need to talk to you again."

Jan was aware Seeward was in no hurry to leave once they were outside Peck's apartment.

"So, what's bothering you?" she said.

"I think we should have a look inside his car."

"The warrant only covers his apartment."

"I'll bet he doesn't know that."

"Possibly, but his attorney will." Jan paused by the passenger-side door to their car. "I'm surprised you would even suggest such a thing."

"Yeah, well."

"Yeah, well what?"

"Jan, I'm tired of these fancy suits and self-entitled jerks thinking they can do whatever they want and not be held accountable."

"So am I, but that doesn't mean we should sidestep procedure just to make an arrest."

"Jan, he's guilty. We know it, and he knows it. If we go back inside and push him harder, he'll crack."

"Seeward, if we do that, and his lawyer finds out, it will factor against Peck being found guilty. I'm not willing to take that risk. Now relax. We'll get him."

Her partner muttered something she couldn't hear and opened the driver's side door.Jan slid into the front seat next to him. "Besides, I want to wait to see if Forensics uncovers any prints on the crowbar I found."

She had the feeling something else was on his mind and understood badgering him for the answer would accomplish nothing, and probably result in an argument. Better to let him tell her in his own time.

CHAPTER 8

Jan sat at her desk, staring at the computer monitor, her arms folded, deep in thought. Like some of their previous cases, this one would not let her rest. A feeling she and her partner may have happened upon the perpetrator while executing a search warrant was not bringing her any satisfaction. Sometimes luck played a part in revealing the identity of a killer, but not often. The discovery of the crucifix in Daniel Peck's apartment had been too easy. Luck may have played a part, but a blindfolded rookie cop walking backwards could have found the piece of jewelry. Even Seeward agreed. Granted, Peck did look and smell like he'd had a night of unconstrained celebration when they first interviewed him. In theory, he could have forgotten to dispose of the necklace. But seldom was any killer dumb enough to hide evidence in his home unless he possessed a troubled mind and the need to keep a souvenir. Peck was a CPA. If he had actually killed Janie Ballentine, then intelligence alone would dictate he discard anything that might be incriminating. Tossing the crucifix down a storm drain or some other out-of-the-way location would have been the wisest move.

Jan had learned early in her career to trust her instincts, and this time her gut was telling her something was wrong. Very wrong.

Noticing she hadn't said a word for several minutes, Seeward eased his chair around the side of his desk. "Are you okay, Jan?"

"Yeah. I was just thinking."

"That's unusual for you so late in the day, isn't it?"

"Ha. Ha. You should take your act on the road."

"Anything you'd like to toss around?"

"Not really. We've been over this case a hundred times already."

Seeward sighed. "Jan, I know Peck told us he was drunk the night he was with Janie Ballentine. And I know he said he couldn't remember half of what they said or did, but he admitted to being with her on the beach."

"And the time of death puts him there as well, according to what he told us. I get it. But he could be wrong about the time he left her condo. I'm starting to think he actually was as messed up as he says."

"Well, I'm tired of hearing that worn-out excuse. The crucifix is the key. Which reminds me, I need to check with Forensics to see if they found any prints."

"They only found a partial print on the pry bar."

"Yeah, but it fit the impression of the wound on the back of Janie Ballantine's head. At least we have the murder weapon."

"Maybe, but it wasn't enough of a print to confirm a match. We still don't know who killed her or why."

Seeward sighed. "Look, Jan, here's what I think happened. Ballantine and Peck went for a walk on the beach. Sometime during their stroll, they got into an argument. He got really pissed and grabbed her by the throat. She fought him off and he ripped the crucifix from around her neck. She tried to get away, he chased her, they fought again, and he popped her in the head with the pry bar."

"Why would he be carrying a pry bar?"

"Jan, I'm simply presenting what I believe to be a possible chain of events."

"How many people do you know carry a pry bar when they go for a walk on the beach?"

"All right, suppose *she* brought it along for protection.

Something she did whenever she walked alone on the beach at night."

Jan shook her head. "Now you're being ridiculous."

"If Peck was as drunk as he says, maybe Ballantine was afraid he might attack her."

"Come on, Seeward, she would carry Mace if she was carrying anything. And if she really *was* afraid he might try something, she would have called a cab and sent him home right away."

"Yeah, I suppose you're right."

"Besides, she'd been with him before when he was drunk. She knew how he would act. I don't believe she was afraid of him. I'm starting to think someone else might have killed her."

"Look, Jan, you're right in saying someone else may have killed her. But you found the murder weapon near the crime scene, and we found her crucifix in his apartment. Peck admitted to being with her on the beach and not remembering everything that happened. I know even if his prints are discovered on the crucifix, it doesn't prove he killed her, but Willie Crain was convicted with very little evidence."

"Willie Crain?"

"The crab trapper and convicted child molester who killed the daughter of an acquaintance. And they never found her body. As far as I'm concerned, Daniel Peck is guilty. And I'm betting if they get him on the stand, he'll crack and confess to killing her."

"Seeward, the simple fact is we need more proof. You know conjecture isn't going to be enough for an arrest." She paused. "I'm beat. Let's sleep on it. We'll talk to David and Darlene Ballantine tomorrow and see if they can give us more to go on."

CHAPTER 9

The next morning, the sight of the Ballantine's spacious and well-tended home in Snell Isle didn't impress Jan in the least. She had interviewed individuals whose lifestyle boasted of their fortune and fame in the past. Having notified David Ballantine of their wish to speak to him and his wife, they entered a residence that emitted an atmosphere steeped in depression.

Wearing a dark blue terrycloth bathrobe, gray slacks, and brown slippers that looked fresh out of the box, Ballantine led them to a chamber lined with bookshelves and four overstuffed chairs facing one another atop a wall-to-wall carpet. Though dignified in appearance, the attorney wore an expression of sorrow, his glazed over eyes and the bouquet of alcohol surrounding him suggested he'd been drinking.

"We were hoping to speak with your wife too, Mr. Ballantine," Jan said.

"She's not feeling well. She's been bedridden ever since... ever since."

"And you?"

Ballantine tendered a frosty stare. "What is it you wish to know, Detective?"

"You told me a little bit about Daniel Peck the last time I saw you. What else can you tell me?"

"Didn't you interview him?"

"Yes, sir."

"I presume you performed a background check."

"We did."

"And the search is ongoing," Seeward said.

"Then what do you want from me?" Ballantine folded his arms.

"Your personal perspective," Jan said. "How did you feel about him dating your daughter?"

"I thought I made that clear."

"I gathered you weren't happy with his position on the food chain, but was there something about him specifically you didn't like?"

Ballantine started to speak, then sighed. "As I believe I mentioned before, we, Darlene and I, didn't dislike Daniel. Personally, I never gave him a second thought. He was well-mannered whenever he and Janie stopped by. And he treated her, and us, with the utmost respect. He always seemed nervous, though. Like he was afraid of us."

"You and your wife?"

"Yes. I just wished he'd acted more like a man."

"Did your daughter ever mention any fights she had with him? Did he ever become violent around her?"

"She never mentioned anything to me. She wouldn't."

"You weren't close with your daughter?"

"I was *very* close with my daughter."

"She wouldn't have told you if Peck had a drinking problem?"

"Some things Janie would only discuss with her mother. Darlene would have told me if there was that kind of trouble between Janie and Daniel." Ballantine paused, his vacant eyes never leaving Jan. "Does this sudden interest in Daniel mean you've uncovered something?"

"We're simply exploring all possibilities, Mr. Ballantine."

"Save the bullshit for the media, Detective. Tell me."

Seeward shifted in his chair.

"Did your daughter wear a crucifix?" Jan said.

"Yes, it was a gift from her best friend, Barbie Davies."

"Barbie Davies?"

"Barbara Susan Davies. She and Janie grew up together."

"Do you know where she lives?"

"In Old Northeast somewhere, but I believe I once heard Janie say she worked for InnFinder."

Seeward pulled a notepad and pen from his coat pocket, and scribbled down the woman's name and the name of the business.

"I'm sure your daughter owns more than one necklace,." Jan said.

"Darlene and I gave her two or three, and she bought several more, but she seemed to prefer the one Barbie gave her. She seldom took it off."

"There was bruising and a laceration on your daughter's neck."

Ballantine nodded. "One of the first things I noticed when you asked me to identify her body."

"We found a crucifix on a broken chain in Daniel Peck's apartment."

Ballantine's eyes widened.

"We're waiting on the report from Forensics to see if there were any fingerprints on it."

"What other evidence have you found?"

"Nothing."

"That's all you've got?"

"A man who lives in your daughter's condo saw two people walking to the beach that night," Seeward said, "but he couldn't positively identify them."

"So, you have nothing," Ballantine said.

Seeward glanced at Jan.

"We found a pry bar near the crime scene," she said. "A partial print was removed from it."

"A partial print that does you no good whatsoever."

"The shape of the pry bar fits the wound on your daughter's

head. We believe it to be the murder weapon."

"You realize every bit of what you've told me is circumstantial."

"Is there anyone you can think of who might have wanted to hurt your daughter?" Jan said.

"No one I know. And that is something Janie would have told both Darlene and me."

"Has anyone you've ever convicted threatened to get back at you by harming your family?"

"They didn't go public with the threat if they did." Ballantine paused. "What is it you're not telling me?"

"Nothing, sir."

"Just speculating, Detective?"

"It's best to consider every possible motive." Jan offered a tight smile. "I believe that's all the questions we have for now, Mr. Ballantine. We still would like to speak with your wife. When she gets to feeling better, would you call us?"

Ballantine nodded.

Jan and Seeward got to their feet, but Ballantine remained seated.

"See yourselves out, will you?" he said.

The brilliance of the sun did little to alter the somber mood of the detectives as they cleared the archway over the front porch. The trek down the gray travertine driveway felt as wearisome to Jan as their investigation. She climbed into their car, but didn't fasten her seat belt and stared straight out the windshield.

Seeward waited a few seconds. "Thinking about how modest Ballantine's house is compared to the rest of the neighborhood, Jan?"

"I don't think Daniel Peck is our killer."

Seeward huffed. "Just because we're short on evidence doesn't mean we should rule him out."

"I'm not ruling him out, but I think there's something else going on."

"Is that why you asked Ballantine about someone wanting to get back at him?"

"I can't help but feel there's something we haven't factored into the mix."

"Like what?"

"What reason, other than a drunk, abusive boyfriend, could have gotten Janie Ballantine killed?"

"How much time do I have?"

Jan eased her head around. "I'm not joking. Suppose the motive *was* revenge. Or payback for a decision that resulted in a company's financial ruin."

"Getting revenge for an unfavorable court decision is not unheard of."

"Exactly. They're both lawyers. You can't tell me there aren't some ex-cons who want to get back at the district attorney. And who knows what course of action a corporate lawyer might have recommended to her bosses that may have left some companies close to bankruptcy."

"But killing their daughter is pretty brazen, not to mention the risk involved. And the ones behind it would have to know every means available would be used to find them."

"Unless there was a lack of evidence and the investigators were focusing on her drunken boyfriend."

"You're saying Daniel Peck is being set up? By whom?"

"Someone brazen enough and willing to take the risk." Jan paused, thinking. "Let's go talk to Peck again. Only this time, let's see if we can convince him to help us."

Jan fastened her seat belt as Seeward started the car and pulled out of the driveway.

CHAPTER 10

During their ride to Daniel Peck's apartment, Jan contacted the homicide office and received word Barbara Susan Davies lived on Cherry Street Northeast, two blocks from the bridge leading into Snell Isle. No address existed for InnFinder, but her home phone number was available.

"Seeward, what type of business is InnFinder, anyway?"

"It's another online company offering the best prices for hotels and motels around the country. You thinking of taking a vacation?"

"Maybe after we close this case."

The first thing Jan and Seeward noticed when they walked into Daniel Peck's apartment was the absence of sand on the floor. He'd cleaned himself up as well, looking more like he belonged behind a desk in an office. The shocked expression on his face told a different story.

"Are you going to arrest me?" he said.

"No, Mr. Peck," Jan said. "We just have a few more questions."

Peck gestured her to the sofa and sat down on the opposite end. Seeward sat in the chair.

"I would never do anything to hurt Janie. I loved her."

"You've made that very clear, Mr. Peck. A witness reported seeing two people headed to the beach early that same morning. I know you said you were drunk and can only remember bits and pieces after you returned to Ms. Ballantine's condo, but I want you to think hard. Could that have been you and Ms. Ballantine on the walkover?"

"I *have* been doing a lot of thinking, Detective. And I'm certain we went to the beach. And I remember a cool breeze and Janie holding me."

"Holding you?"

"Helping me, I guess."

"But you don't remember arguing?"

"Not right then. But as I told you, she was mad at me because I'd drunk too much at the club. She drove us back to her place and let me know she was unhappy the whole way."

"So, you did argue."

"Not in the car."

"While you were drinking coffee, maybe?"

"I was a having a strange dream when you came by the first time."

"When you stubbed your toe."

"At that time, I thought we were arguing in my dream. I was really hungover. But the more I thought about it... it may have been on the beach."

"What were you arguing about?"

Peck paused. "That part I still can't remember."

"How long did you argue?"

"I don't know, but I think she got mad and walked off. I can't be sure, though."

"We checked the cab companies, Uber, Lyft, and the other ridesharing companies for that day and time of the morning," Seeward said. "Your name didn't appear on any customer lists."

"Then I guess I drove myself home."

"Take a moment and relax, Mr. Peck," Jan said. "Then I want you to concentrate."

They waited as Peck inhaled twice, releasing long, slow breaths.

"Okay," he said.

"Do you recall seeing anyone else on the beach or around Ms. Ballantine's condo before you left?"

Peck shook his head.

"No one entering or pulling out of 132nd Avenue?"

"I don't even remember getting into my car."

"At any time, did Ms. Ballantine ever mention anyone threatening her?"

"Janie was easy to like, Detective, and even easier to get to know. If someone had a problem with her, it was because they were envious."

"But no one you can think of offhand."

"She was smart enough to recognize those types and stay away from them."

"I believe that's all we have," Mr. Peck.

The accountant stood up as Jan and Seeward got to their feet. "I'll do my best to remember all Janie and I did that night. I want to know who killed her as much as you do."

Seeward was unusually quiet as their car rolled up to Seminole Boulevard.

Jan was lost in thought. Daniel Peck's honesty strengthened her belief he was telling the truth. His willingness to speak to them without a lawyer present made accepting his recollections as true much easier. And their investigation more difficult. She glanced at her partner.

"Still think he did it?" she said.

"Yep."

"He seemed more cooperative once we told him he wasn't going to be arrested."

"And he had plenty of time to dream up that bilge."

"You think he's that good at fabricating a story?"

"I think when people fear for their lives, they're capable of doing anything."

"He didn't hesitate to open up. Even volunteered some answers."

"Uh-huh. But he's still playing the sympathy card. And by the way, he told us nothing. Again."

"All right, I admit we've come across others who've played the same game and turned out to be as guilty as the day is long. But this guy doesn't feel right for it to me."

"Jan, I know better than to dispute your gut feeling. You're right more often than not. But what little evidence and testimony we have points to Peck, albeit circumstantial. And until we find something which points us in a different direction, nothing is going to change my mind."

"You're a stubborn man, Seeward Sinclair."

Seeward grinned. "I got it from my partner."

CHAPTER 11

A look of disgust covered Jan's face after her call to Barbara Davies went to voicemail. She left a short message.

"We'll wait five minutes, and if she doesn't get back to us, I'll call again."

Jan's phone rang while still in her hand.

"Detective Larkin, this is Barbara Davies."

"Ms. Davies, we need to speak with you in regard to an investigation we're conducting. We'd like to see you as soon as possible."

"Oh! Yes, of course. I guess today would be all right."

"Do you still work for InnFinder?"

"Yes."

"May I have the office address?"

"I work from home. Is this about Janie Ballantine?"

"It is. Are you still living on Cherry Street Northeast?"

"Yes."

"We had an interview in Seminole and are about to cross the Bay Pines bridge, so it'll be a few minutes before we get there."

Seeward kept up with the flow of traffic and steered them down Tyrone Boulevard to 22nd Avenue and turned left.

"I sure hope this trip is worth it," he said.

"You already know the answer. It's a fifty-fifty deal."

"We'll be wasting our time if *Barbie* turns out to be a bubble brain."

"What brought this on?"

"We know David and Darlene Ballantine are intelligent and have built successful careers. And their daughter has two master's degrees. How did Janie wind up becoming friends with Barbie? I mean, how smart do you have to be to list a group of prices for your customers to decide which one is the best deal?"

"You're being awfully judgmental."

"I don't know. Maybe it's because we've run into so many dead ends."

"Dead ends are nothing new. I agree this case has a boat-load. Let's hope this interview brings us some luck."

Staying positive during the worst moments was difficult at times. Both she and Seeward had needed an attitude boost at one time or another during their association. Nothing more was said until they turned onto Cherry Street. An absence of cars on the two-lane street made locating Barbara Davies' home a simple task.

"I believe it's the next one on the right," Jan said.

"Got it. And I'm glad we don't have to walk too far."

The house consisted of red bricks and had a chimney. Limited foliage dressed the front and sides of the Bahia lawn, and foxtail palms lined the right-of-way.

Seeward rang the doorbell and shifted his focus to across the street.

Seconds later, the dark mahogany door opened.

The color of her hair and eyes was the only exception to Barbara Davies being a match to Janie Ballantine. She was the same height as her friend, with long, straight auburn hair to her shoulders, drawing attention to a face blessed with emerald eyes and milky skin. She wore a tentative expression.

"I'm Detective Sinclair and this is Detective Sergeant Larkin, Pinellas County Sheriff's Office," Seeward said before Jan could speak.

Davies' expression eased. "Please come in."

She led them through a living room with the usual middle-class amenities: a floral sofa fronted by a coffee table strewn with magazines, faux leather recliner, and a single floor lamp occupying the far corner. Passing by a modest-sized kitchen, they found themselves inside a wood-paneled Florida room.

"The couch is comfortable," Davies said, pointing to a rattan sofa against the wall. She took a seat in a black office chair in front of a computer desk.

As she and Seeward sat down, Jan gazed at the twin lamp tables on either end of the sofa, withholding a smile when she noticed the woman had captured her partner's attention.

"Now, Ms. Davies," she said, "first let me say how sorry I am. I understand you and Ms. Ballantine had known each other for quite some time."

"Since elementary school. It was like our friendship was destined to happen."

"You knew her well then."

"We were sisters. That's how we felt about each other."

"Growing up, did she have many boyfriends?"

"Oh, yes. From middle school right on through college."

"You two were together the entire time?"

"Not in college. I went to St. Petersburg College. Janie went to USF. Her parents wanted her to go to Gainesville, their alma mater, but she wanted to stay close to home."

"To be near Daniel Peck?"

"She didn't know him then. She was dating a guy in the Air Force stationed at MacDill."

"Do you remember his name?"

"Tommy English. Thomas, I guess. I don't know if Thomas was his first name or his middle name."

Jan nodded. "How did they get along?"

"Pretty good at first. He was funny. They had a bad argument right before she broke it off."

"Do you know what they were arguing about?"

"He was getting ready to be reassigned and proposed to her. She wasn't looking to get married."

"Then he's no longer at MacDill."

"He's in Germany, I think. I really don't know."

"Did she date many guys after that before she met Daniel Peck?"

"None. She met Danny at a party, and that was it. They've been together for two years." Davies lowered her eyes. "I should say they *were* together for two years."

"Have you ever seen them argue?"

"Sure. What couple doesn't? But Janie told me they didn't argue very often. She loved he was so agreeable."

"I understand he drank a lot."

"That's not true. I don't know why anyone would have told you that. Janie said he did sometimes, but he didn't overdo it."

"Do you know if he ever hit her?"

"No way!" Davies narrowed her eyes. "Janie wouldn't put up with that shit. You know who her father is, right?"

"When was the last time you saw her?"

"I don't remember exactly, but I spoke with her three days before..." Davies lowered her eyes again. "She and Danny had been spending a lot of time together."

"When you last spoke with her, did she happen to mention if she was having trouble with anyone? Someone following her, maybe?"

"No, Janie did her best to avoid any kind of trouble. She was a good and kind-hearted person. All of us who knew her liked her very much."

"Thank you for your time, Ms. Davies, and again—"

"We're sorry for your loss," Seeward said.

Davies appeared in no hurry to resume working as they left the room.

Once they'd climbed into their car, Jan set her eyes on her partner. His staring straight ahead told her his mind was somewhere else. And she knew why.

"She certainly presented a strong defense for Daniel Peck," Jan said.

"Yeah."

"It was close to sounding personal. Like she might be attracted to him."

"Could be, I suppose."

"Kind of makes you wonder though, doesn't it?"

Seeward swung his head around. "Wonder what?"

"If she's been to his place to console him."

"Maybe. It sounded to me like they were friends."

"Maybe more than friends."

"I don't think so."

"Why not? What's wrong with a friend helping a friend in need?"

"She's doesn't seem like the type. Not the way you mean."

"And what type is that?"

"Someone who takes advantage of a person when they're most vulnerable."

Jan shrugged. "You could be right."

"Yeah."

"But she's your type, isn't she?"

"What? Get outta here."

"Wipe the drool off your chin."

Seeward glanced in the rearview mirror.

Jan laughed.

"You're real funny."

"I saw the way you looked at her when she opened the door. You couldn't wait to introduce yourself."

Seeward grinned. "She *is* beautiful."

"Don't go getting any ideas, partner...not until we're through with this case."

CHAPTER 12

A message from Forensics was waiting for Jan and Seeward once they returned to the office. Like most everything involved with their case, the news wasn't good.

"No prints found on the crucifix, Jan," Seeward said. "No sand either."

Jan growled and folded her arms as she sat back in her chair. She was frustrated by the growing sense they would never solve the case. Exhausting all avenues of possibility seemed a meager reward for failure.

"You would have thought some sand was embedded in the chain links. Or skin. Hair. Some kind of DNA but, according to the report, it was clean."

"Well, something made that bruise on Janie Ballantine's neck," Jan said.

"She had several necklaces in her bedroom when I went through it. But there was no way to tell if one of them was missing."

"Guess we'd better talk to the Ballantines again."

The phone on Jan's desk rang. Her scowl deepened. She took a second to constrain her discontent and picked up the receiver.

"Detective Larkin, my name is Karen Trudell. I live in the Sea Castle condos in Madeira Beach. I just got back into town last night and heard about Janie Ballantine when I ran into one of my neighbors this morning. I thought I should call you."

"Yes, Ms. Trudell. How can I help you?"

"I don't know if this means anything, but a couple of days before I left town, I saw a man looking at the building directory in front of the office. I'm not sure, but he might have been visiting one of my neighbors. I know he wasn't a resident."

"You'd never seen this man before?"

"He was a stranger to me. Very handsome, I must say, but kind of scary, too."

Jan's eyes darted to Seeward, but she was unable to attract his attention. He was busy working on his computer. She reached across her desk for her notepad and pen. "Do you remember any specifics about what he looked like?"

"Absolutely. As I passed by him, I dropped my valise. He was kind enough to pick it up for me. He was tall, six feet or more, I'd say. I guess he weighed, oh, around two hundred pounds. And his taste in clothes was superb."

"Do you recall anything about his features? His hair? His eyes?"

"He had black hair and blue eyes. Steely blue eyes like…like he was merciless. That's what made him kind of scary looking. But his smile…his smile was to die for. Oh! I guess I shouldn't have said that."

"That's okay, Ms. Trudell. You're doing fine." Jan scribbled down the information.

"And he was *very* polite."

"You said he was well dressed. Do you recall what was he wearing?"

"A dark gray suit and a black dress shirt opened up. Oh, and black shoes. His shoes looked expensive."

"Anything else you can remember?"

"Let me think…No, I don't believe so."

Seeward chose that moment to wheel his chair from in front of his computer monitor and stretch.

Jan waved and drew his attention "And you say you'd never seen this man around your condo before?"

"That's right. Oh, wait! Wait! I'm pretty sure he drove a black Porsche. I remember because I saw one in our parking lot. We have a small lot and I know every one of my neighbors' cars. The Porsche had to be his."

"By any chance, did you get the tag number?"

The woman's voice dropped off. "No. I'm sorry."

"Would you mind coming into the office so we can work up a composite sketch of this man? It would help us a great deal."

"I'll be there as soon as I can."

Jan hung up the phone and set her eyes on her partner.

"What was that all about?" he asked.

"Ms. Karen Trudell, who lives in the same condo as Janie Ballantine, saw a stranger checksing out the building directory a couple of days before she went out of town."

"Karen Trudell?" Seeward grabbed his notepad and flipped through the pages. "So, that explains why she wasn't home when I was interviewing her neighbors the morning Ballantine was discovered." He moved his chair closer. "Did she tell you anything that might help us?"

Jan shoved her notes toward him.

Seeward picked up the notepad and gave it a going over.

"Pretty good memory for someone who just got back into town, huh?"

"You're telling me," he said and flipped the notepad onto her desk. Wheeling his chair back to his computer, he clacked away on the keyboard a few seconds, pausing before a broad smile appeared on his face. "Take a look at this, Jan."

Jan rose from her chair, rounded her desk, and stood next to him.

On the front page of the *Tampa Bay Times* was a picture of Colby Rittenhouse as he was leaving the Pinellas County courthouse. Wearing an arrogant expression of triumph, he was a free man once more after having beaten all the charges against him. Behind him stood a handsome man with dark hair and blue eyes, wearing a dark gray coat.

Jan leaned forward for a closer look as a familiar tingling swept through her. A feeling she sometimes experienced when working cases in the past. A corridor through adversity was about to open. The man fit the description given her by Karen Trudell.

"What do you think, Jan?"

"Find out who he is and let's pay him a visit."

CHAPTER 13

Jan had read about Edward Papalos, the Rittenhouse body-guard, in the past and before Seeward's search confirmed his identity. "Eddie" had an extensive relationship with the law. Assault, battery, armed robbery, and suspicion of murder were his claims to infamy. No convictions pointed to him or an accomplice possessing the intelligence to remove all traces of his association with the crimes. Or, possibly, residing behind the curtain of influence provided by his boss helped to secure his freedom. A supposition strongly supported by the fact his last known address was the residence of Colby Rittenhouse. Armed with this knowledge, she and Seeward constructed a theory as to what they believed may have happened to Janie Ballantine.

Before the trial of Colby Rittenhouse began, it was a fore-gone conclusion David Ballantine would act as lead attorney.

And rather than prolonging the battle in court and risk losing the case, Jan thought, *someone close to the crime boss came up with a quicker solution.* "What better way to disrupt the trial than to have someone in Ballantine's family mur-dered?" she said to herself.

Killing the district attorney would immediately point a suspicious finger at Rittenhouse. Doing away with his wife, Darlene Ballantine, an all-star in the world of corporate law, could give rise to a similar amount of supposition. But their daughter, known only in select circles around the county, retained a degree of anonymity. She would be the better candidate. And given Papalos's relationship with Rittenhouse, it was easy to conclude he had been selected to do the job. Proving it, however, was not so simple a task.

Karen Trudell arrived a short time later and greeted the detectives with a welcoming smile. A diminutive, stocky woman with fiery red hair and spirited blue eyes, she was accompanied by a thin, teenage African American girl.

"Who is your friend, Ms. Trudell?" Jan asked.

"This is Shanice Franklin. She's the daughter of a friend and co-worker at the bank where I work. I'd forgotten her mother and I had decided to do lunch today when I told you I'd come down here. Shanice came with her mother."

Jan noticed the girl was holding a drawing pad a few inches larger than a sheet of paper. "What have you got there, Shanice?"

The girl's smile glistened with perfect white teeth. "I drew a picture of the man Ms. Trudell saw at her condo."

"She's an artist," Trudell said. "And she's very good."

"I'm sure she is," Jan said, "but I would prefer you get with our sketch artist. No offense, Shanice."

"I think you should see her drawing first, Detective Larkin."

Never losing her smile, Franklin flipped the cover and held out the pad.

"This almost looks like a photograph," Seeward said.

The features of the man's face were crafted with the utmost precision and skillfully detailed. A most impressive reproduction.

"He looked exactly like that," Trudell said.

"We're going to need the drawing, Shanice," Jan said.

"Of course." She ripped the page from the pad and handed it to Jan.

"Detective, run a search of this, please."

Seeward took the drawing to his desk and went to work on his computer.

"I believe that's all we need, Ms. Trudell. Thank you for stopping by."

"My pleasure, Detective."

"And thank you for your assistance, Shanice."

"You're welcome, Detective Larkin."

"We certainly could use someone with your skill in the sheriff's office. Have you thought about what you would like to do once you finish school?"

"I'm hoping to get a college scholarship and continue to perfect my work. I want to become a professional artist."

"I'm certain you'll succeed. You're very talented."

After they had gone, Jan walked over to Seeward's desk. He was comparing the drawing to the photo of the Rittenhouse bodyguard in the *Tampa Bay Times*. Smiles covered both their faces when they concluded the match was dead on. An unannounced meeting with Eddie Papalos would top their list of things to do the following day.

CHAPTER 14

Feeling as though she needed to relax before going home, Jan pulled out of the parking lot and drove to Seminole Boulevard. A right turn pointed her in the direction of the coast and several small bars to which she was acquainted.

Approaching the separation of roads to the beaches and the area known as Bay Pines, Jan held to a westerly course until she reached the Tom Stuart Causeway. Navigating the bridge over the Intracoastal Waterway would land her in Madeira Beach. At the causeway's end, she turned south on Gulf Boulevard, happy as the pace of traffic picked up, and even more at ease when the traffic thinned out. She made it a point not to stare as she passed by the street leading to Janie Ballantine's condo. This was her personal time to enjoy.

Once she'd traversed the John's Pass Bridge into Treasure Island, she remembered an establishment she'd frequented a few times in the past and hoped it was still open for business. The Spinnaker Bar and Grill had been a haven for many older blue-collar locals. To the winter visitors who made their yearly return to the small community on the Gulf coast, it held all the warmth and friendliness of a favorite bar in their hometown. Jan liked the unpretentious watering hole because it was small and personable. And the more mature patrons were not so rambunctious.

Happy to find a parking space the moment she arrived, Jan

walked into the dimly lit barroom and noticed only a few customers sitting here and there. The layout was simple. Five booths lined the wall on the right with a half dozen tables scattered about the floor. The stained mahogany bar along the left wall hosted a dozen bar chairs. In lieu of a band, an ancient jukebox sitting alone against the far wall provided the entertainment. Most of the selections were instrumentals and ballads from the 50's and early 60's which never changed because the owner wanted it that way. The jukebox was seldom used unless a customer was feeling sentimental.

A previous visit had Jan feeling sorry for herself, so she'd selected D-17. Claiming one of the booths, she stared into her beer while Andy Williams sang "The Days of Wine and Roses." The song was one of ex-husband Ken's favorites. They used to dance to the number each time they had the opportunity. Finding it difficult to control her emotions while sitting by herself, the company of other patrons had kept her from crying.

Ken had never raised his voice when teasing her about her unkempt ways. He made her laugh, and her love for him ran deep in a time she thought was the happiest in her life—until he confessed their arrangement was not his idea of what a marriage should be. In an effort to save their relationship, they opened up to one another about their personal feelings, even sought professional counseling, but they could never reach a mutual agreement. Their parting had been amicable, but she was heartbroken.

Overcoming the disappointment took considerable time, but she was a strong-willed woman and was able to gain peace of mind. She accepted the harsh realization only a special kind of person could endure being married to a cop, and she vowed never again to allow a man to stand between her and her profession.

The atmosphere tonight was perfect, and she concluded the very last booth would be the ideal nesting place. As she skirted alongside of the other booths, she glanced to her left toward the bar. Spying a familiar face sitting in one of the bar chairs, she immediately changed direction.

Sliding into a chair next to the old soul seated at the end of the bar, she wasn't surprised when he didn't acknowledge her presence.

"Buy a girl a drink, sailor?" she said.

Slowly turning and eying her through a permanent squint, the man of the sea released a disapproving snort. "Buy yer own damn drink, Cap'um."

His salty comeback made Jan smile. "Guess I've lost my touch."

"Hank!" the old salt bellowed. "A drink fer the lady!"

Quite a few years had passed since a man had called her a lady. Sergeant, detective, or simply woman was more often the offering. At least it seemed like a long time to her.

Jan was surprised and flattered. "Shot of whiskey and a beer, please," she said to the bartender.

Crabby Phillips, the old man she'd encountered on the beach behind Janie Ballantine's condo, leveled a look of mild astonishment.

"Figured you ta be a wino." He took in more of his beer. "Ya don't eat kwish, do ya?"

Jan laughed out loud. "No, Crabby. I hate quiche."

Crabby smiled, his stained yellow teeth encircled by his snow-white beard. "So, how ya been?"

"Not too bad." She sighed. "Actually, some days are good, some not so much."

"We all has 'em."

"You seem pretty even tempered."

"That's because you don't know him that well," the bartender said. Hank placed a shot and beer in front of her.

"Ain't you got nothin' better ta do?" Crabby said.

Hank winked at Jan and left to see to a customer at the other end of the bar.

Jan scooped up the shot of whiskey, drank it, then chased it with a generous pull of beer. A couple of minutes passed.

"That thing with the girl not goin' so good?" he asked.

"Not as well as I'd like."

"Too bad."

"Well, you win some, you lose some, and some get rained out."

Crabby grinned as he studied his mug. "You like ta go fishin'?"

"Yeah. I guess so. I haven't been in a long time, though."

Crabby downed the last of his brew and waved his mug. "Hank!" he bellowed.

When Crabby turned to her, Jan observed the tired look in his brown eyes.

"Sometimes when I gets fed up with people, I takes muh boat way out in the Gulf. I drops the anchor, tosses outta line, an' sits back an' fergits all about 'em. Don't matter if I don't catch nothin'. It's mighty peaceable out there. Gits me back on course. Yer welcome aboard any time ya like."

Jan smiled. "Thank you. I'll remember that."

The fact the old geezer was kind enough to extend the offer eased the tension of her busy day. Proving Eddie Papalos had killed Janie Ballantine would be a formidable job with the odds stacked against her and Seeward. Tonight, though, she would take pleasure in an evening with her new acquaintance. She would ask him to recount some of his many sea-going adventures and hoped he would oblige. Losing herself in his colorful fish tales was what she needed to get back on course.

CHAPTER 15

Jan wished every morning could be as pleasant as this beautiful day. The sun was shining in a near cloudless sky, the humidity low. Others sharing the road with her seemed to benefit from the same sentiment. Even the traffic lights worked in her favor. Her ride to work was actually enjoyable.

Her chance meeting with Crabby Phillips at the Spinnaker Bar and Grill had been memorable. The old tar was a great storyteller. Whether or not his stories were true didn't matter. His dry sense of humor and colloquial manner of speaking had her doubled over with laughter throughout the evening. She laughed out loud when she recalled one of his funnier stories and vowed to spend more evenings at the Spinnaker.

Her phone rang and forced her out of the moment. Thinking the call might be work-related, she pushed the hands-free button on the steering wheel.

"Jan, it's Seeward."

Her cheery mood returned. "Seeward, you hot looking hunk of man! How *are* you this fine, fine morning?"

"I'm fine, Jan. You sound like you're in a good mood. You're not drunk, are you?"

"Of course not. What's on your mind?"

"David Ballantine called. He wants to talk to you right away."

"Ballantine? Did he give you any idea of what he wanted?"

"No, but he sounded serious."

"He always sounds serious. I wonder why he's calling me, though."

"Maybe after our last visit, he was taken in by the old Larkin charm."

"Stop it."

"Seriously, Jan, I think you'd better get back to him. And soon."

Seeward passed along Ballantine's phone number.

Curiosity began to make her itch. Ballantine could have spoken directly to the lieutenant to find out how their case was progressing. He probably wanted to hear the details straight from her. And he wouldn't be happy with what little she had to tell him.

Once she'd found an empty space in the sheriff's office parking lot, she pondered the conversation that would soon take place with the district attorney. She released a long, slow breath of air in anticipation of the impending interrogation and fought to quell her anxiety as she punched in his number.

"Jan, how are you?" Ballantine said.

"Fine, sir."

"Let's drop the formalities, shall we? Please call me David."

His unexpected candor surprised her. "Okay. What can I do for you, David?"

"I'd like you to come by the house. I have an important matter I wish to discuss with you."

"Certainly. We were planning to do an interview today, but I'm sure we can earmark a time that's convenient for you."

"How about right now?"

Jan blinked several times. "Okay. Let me get a hold of my partner, and we'll—"

"I want you to come alone, Jan."

"Uh...sure. Let me check in, and I'll be right over."

What matter could be so important, and why the urgent need to discuss it with her? Had he become privy to the same information regarding Eddie Papalos she and Seeward had uncovered? Or was it something else? She picked up her phone.

"What's up, Jan? You stuck in traffic?"

"No, Seeward, I'm sitting in the parking lot."

"Anything wrong?"

"Not at the moment. Why?"

"I don't know. You sound like something's bothering you."

"I just had an interesting conversation with David Ballantine."

"Oh? What did he want?"

"He wants me to come over to his place right now."

"Did he say why?"

"Something important he wants to discuss."

"Do you think he knows about Eddie Papalos?"

"The thought occurred to me, but I'm not so sure."

"Okay, I'll get the car and meet you in the lot."

"He wants me to come alone."

"Now that's weird."

"Why? I've spoken directly to him and the A.D.A. in regard to cases before."

"But not at their homes."

"True. Look, I'll call you after I've finished with him. Keep up your search on Eddie Papalos."

"Got it. I'll be interested to hear what Ballantine has to tell you...not to mention curious."

Jan wondered what was on David Ballantine's mind as well.

CHAPTER 16

David Ballantine looked as though he was dressed for an afternoon of golf and cocktails at the country club. Clean-shaven, his short sleeve burgundy polo shirt and tailored black slacks were a dramatic change from the casual bedtime apparel he wore during the last visit. His blue eyes were clear, and he looked ready to resume his rightful place as prosecuting attorney.

He escorted Jan to the same den, and they took seats in the same overstuffed chairs facing one another. He didn't waste a second.

"Would you care for some coffee, Jan?" he said.

"Thank you, David, but I've had my quota for the day."

Ballantine smiled.

"How is your wife doing?"

"Not very well, I'm afraid. She's still bedridden. I brought in a private duty nurse to tend to her needs."

"I'm sorry to hear that."

"Forgive me if I came across as secretive when I asked you to meet me. But what I wish to discuss with you is for your ears only."

Jan nodded.

"It goes without saying I'm extremely unhappy with the outcome of the Rittenhouse trial."

"That was unfortunate. I know you were pushing hard for a conviction."

"We would have finally gotten that son of a... Anyway, I don't suppose you have anything new to tell me in regard to your investigation of the death of my daughter."

"There *has* been a new development we're planning to explore. I wanted to make sure we were on the right track before I contacted you."

"Cut the cop etiquette bullshit, Jan. Talk to me."

Jan took a deep breath and related the entire Karen Trudell interview, the drawing they received from Shanice Franklin, and added her belief Daniel Peck had nothing to do with his daughter's murder. She confided to Ballantine her suspicion of Eddie Papalos, although they had no proof, and paused when she saw his face go flush and anger fill his eyes. Honest in admitting her uncertainty as to how they would go about tying Papalos to the killing, she sat back and allowed him time to regain his composure.

"David, we both know Papalos being at your daughter's condo could be viewed as circumstantial, even with Karen Trudell's testimony and the drawing."

Ballantine exhaled. "I agree with you, Jan. And so there's no misunderstanding, Darlene and I have no ill feelings toward Dan. We don't want to believe he's guilty." Ballantine paused five long seconds. "Jan, I'm going to say something I've never said to any cop before. If it comes back on me, I'll deny it and call you a liar to your face. Understood?"

An icy shard slid down Jan's spine. "I understand."

"If you honestly believe Eddie Papalos is the killer, and you have no other legal recourse at your disposal, then I want you to use whatever means you deem necessary to resolve the problem. Do we understand one another?"

His cloaked suggestion to eliminate Papalos as a means to avenge his daughter's murder stunned her. Not to say she hadn't considered taking matters into her own hands before. But she'd never acted upon it. David Ballantine had an impeccable reputation for being a straight shooter. He had never resorted to or condoned any sort of unlawful tactics.

Jan took a moment to consider her answer. "I understand your desire for resolution, David. It's just I'm not sure that the avenue you're suggesting I take would be prudent or in the best interest of bringing about closure."

"Before you dismiss my proposition, let me add I would be willing to consider a reward for your compliance...say, somewhere in the neighborhood of a six-figure remuneration."

"David, I hope you're not suggesting a bribe. You know I'm bound by law to take action if you make an attempt."

"I'll support to the fullest whatever decision you deem necessary, Jan. You have my word on it."

From past experience and conversations with his associates, Jan knew Ballantine's word was his bond. In all his years on the bar, he'd never once hung a cop out to dry. But as far as she knew, he'd never asked a cop to murder anyone either.

"I'll do my best to bring this matter to an end in a manner that benefits all of us. And you have *my* word on that."

"I know you will, Jan. And thank you."

CHAPTER 17

Jan was of two minds whether she could honor Ballantine's unethical request when she walked into the office. In the past, she'd pondered taking a similar course of action when she and Seeward had determined a man had killed his brother. But evidence supporting their claim was lacking. Watching the murderer go free had been difficult for her to accept, and a bullet seemed the quickest and most efficient method of serving justice. But she couldn't bring herself to even suggest the idea to her partner. Holding fast to the code of honor she had sworn to uphold was sometimes more difficult than most people would like to believe. As she approached her desk, she noticed her partner hard at work. She paused a moment to take a deep breath and prepared herself for the line of questioning soon to follow. "Good morning, Seeward.".

"Good morning, Jan." He stopped what he was doing and looked up. "How'd the meeting go?"

"It didn't take long. Ballantine basically wanted an update on our progress."

"You could have told him that on the phone."

Jan shrugged.

"What did you tell him?"

"Most of what we told him before. Then I explained we'd just heard from Karen Trudell and received a good description of the man seen at his daughter's condo."

"How did he react when you told him it was Eddie Papalos?"

"Obviously, he's not happy with the outcome of the Colby Rittenhouse trial. Learning Papalos had been snooping around her condo made him angry. I thought he was going to have a heart attack. But he agreed with me when I told him Papalos being at his daughter's condo could be viewed as a coincidence."

"Really? I wouldn't see it that way if it were my daughter. Especially if I was trying to prosecute his boss."

"Can you provide any proof the only reason Papalos was there was to find Janie Ballantine?"

Seeward huffed. "No, I guess not. Is that all he had to say?"

"He said he appreciated our effort and had the utmost confidence we would find the killer."

"I thought he had something important to discuss?"

Jan looked down at her desk. "Yeah, well, whatever."

"Maybe it was something else."

"Like what?"

"Like I said before, maybe he was taken in by the old Larkin charm and just wanted to see you again."

"Would you get off that?"

Seeward grinned and went back to work.

"Any new developments this morning?"

Her partner froze.

Jan couldn't help but notice the uncomfortable expression on his face.

"Not really. But I did want to talk to you about...uh..."

"What is it, Seeward?"

"Jan, there's something I need to tell you. Let's talk outside."

The reason for her partner's odd behavior was a mystery to Jan. He had idiosyncrasies like everyone, but she'd never seen him act this way before. She followed him through the Homicide office door and into the corridor.

"I called my buddy, Don Jennings," Seeward said. "He's

with the FBI. I asked him if he would let us know if their mole knew anything about—"

"Mole! What mole?"

"Shh! Jesus, Jan, not so loud. The FBI has a mole inside the Rittenhouse organization. I asked Don if he could get verification Eddie Papalos was ordered to kill Janie Ballantine."

Jan had a terrible feeling Seeward's conversation with Don Jennings had been more in-depth. She hoped she was wrong. "Why in the hell would you ask him to do something like that?"

"Because he owes me. And because we can use the help."

"Owes you? What could you have possibly done for him to warrant…Never mind. I don't want to know."

"Jan, the more we can find out, the better chance we'll have to nail Papalos."

"Have you given any thought to what you've asked him to do? Leaking information to anyone is something the bureau frowns upon."

"I know."

"Your friend could lose his job…or worse."

"He wasn't happy when I pressed him."

"You pressed him?"

"I told him I needed some answers in three days."

"And he agreed?"

"Not at first, so I reminded him of his tendency to brag about being the best agent in the bureau."

Jan shook her head. "Did you push *all* his buttons?"

"He'll come through for us, Jan."

"I want to know the minute he calls with any information."

"Got it."

"Check that. All I want to know is if Papalos did it or not. Nothing else."

"I understand."

"And Seeward, please don't agree to anything you may regret later."

Secretly, Jan was thrilled her partner had found a way for them to confirm what they both believed and maybe solve her problem as well.

CHAPTER 18

Days dragged on, and the unmerciful Florida summer went from sizzling to broiling, bringing out the worst in everyone. The heat and humidity rose along with the frustration weighing on Jan and Seeward. Every attempt to interview Eddie Papalos had been met with a delay. Sickness, vacation, even visiting his ailing mother in upstate New York were the excuses handed to them. A different dodge with each phone call. The one trip they took to Colby Rittenhouse's mansion in south Tampa resulted in the same callous denial. Eddie Papalos wasn't there, and no one knew when he would return.

They revisited the Sea Castle condominiums, showing the drawing of the Rittenhouse bodyguard to all the residents they encountered. They also talked to other homeowners along Gulf Lane, the small street running in front of the condo, and the employees of businesses for five square blocks in either direction. The result was the same. No one recognized or had seen him.

Fred Flannigan, who witnessed two figures on their way to the beach the morning of the murder, was also unable to recognize Papalos but shed some new light on his previous sighting. Inviting Jan and Seeward into his home, the cordial retiree led them to his balcony and roost, where he enjoyed his cigars.

"I'm glad you stopped by," he said. "I was close to calling

you." He pointed to one of two wicker patio chairs. "I was sitting here. As you can tell, I have a pretty good view of the immediate area and most of the walkover. Most people coming from or going to the beach don't even know I'm watching them."

"Even at night?" Jan said.

"I keep the curtains drawn so no one can tell if my wife and I are at home."

"Where is your wife?"

"She's a volunteer for Meals On Wheels. She's a good woman. Anyway, when I'm out here early in the morning, like I was the other time, it's difficult to tell who's on the walkover. Even with a full moon."

"But you said you saw a man and a woman when I interviewed you," Seeward said.

"Right, but only because one of them was wearing a dress. I've been giving it some thought, and I remembered she was hanging onto him because he couldn't walk straight. They kept bumping into the railing. I guess he was drunk or on drugs. I don't know."

"Were they talking?" Jan said.

"They were, but like I told Detective Sinclair, I couldn't make out what they were saying."

"And you're certain the man was struggling to walk a straight line."

"They stopped a few times. It looked to me like she was letting him rest against the railing."

"But they managed to get to the beach."

"They did. I thought for sure he'd fall on his face before they cleared the dunes."

"And you never saw them again."

"After they disappeared, I never saw anyone else before I turned in."

"Detective Sinclair said you heard an argument while you were still out here."

"I did. It was very faint, though. I couldn't make out what they were saying."

"A man and a woman?"

"Sounded like it to me."

"I recall you telling me you didn't know Jane Ballantine," Seeward said.

"I didn't. My wife, neither. We passed her in the parking lot a few times. She was friendly. Very polite and was always smiling when she greeted us."

"But you never saw her boyfriend," Jan said.

"I couldn't begin to tell you what he looked like."

"And you're positive you've never seen anyone who resembles the man in the drawing we showed you."

"I haven't. I'll ask my wife when she gets home. But Detective Larkin, my wife and I keep to ourselves. We don't like people prying into our business and we keep our noses out of theirs."

As Seeward eased their car onto Gulf Boulevard from 132nd Avenue, he released a lengthy sigh. "I was really hoping someone might be able to confirm Karen Trudell's description of Papalos."

"If he's our man, I'm surprised he allowed himself to be seen. To my way of thinking, that's a pretty ignorant thing to do."

"True, unless you have guts enough to think you can get away with being spotted. I mean, we haven't been able to find him. And I'm sure his boss has the best lawyers available lined up to defend him when we do."

"That's a given."

"Fred Flannigan confirmed Daniel Peck's claim he was drunk the entire time he was with Janie Ballantine."

"While they were walking to the beach, anyway, but it still doesn't mean he didn't kill her."

"Now you're starting to sound like me."

Jan said nothing.

By the time they reached Seminole Boulevard, Jan had the

strong sense once again their case was slipping away. And as much as it pained her to admit it, they would have to wait and hope for a break in the case. But while they waited, the search for evidence and witnesses would continue until all existing avenues were exhausted.

Silence accompanied by a somber mood carried Jan and Seeward from the sheriff's office parking lot to the homicide office. The clatter and conversations of other detectives did nothing to shake the unhappiness from them.

Jan was studying the drawing of Eddie Papalos when Seeward rolled his chair up to her desk. He was wearing an expression she had come to recognize over the years. A confidential topic was about to be divulged.

"Jan, I hate to tell you this, but I haven't heard a thing from Don Jennings."

"I gathered as much after the three days were up."

"I've been calling him a lot. Too much, I guess. He's really pissed."

"I can imagine."

"I don't believe he's going to come through for us."

"Sorry to hear that. I know you meant well, but you put him in an awful position."

Seeward nodded.

"I get not solving a case bothers you as much as it bothers me, but I'm curious why you pushed your friend so hard for this one. It's not like you owe David Ballantine anything."

Seeward stared at her.

"Or do you?"

"I'd rather not say."

"Seeward, I'm your partner. Whatever you say will stay between us."

Seconds of silence followed.

"My Uncle Bill," he said.

"Your Uncle Bill?"

"My uncle Bill was hospitalized right before he died. His

kidneys were failing. I didn't get to see him much, but when I did, all he could talk about was this pretty young volunteer who used to come by and cheer him up. He knew he was dying, Jan, but his eyes came alive whenever he spoke of her."

"The volunteer was Janie Ballantine, right?"

"Her being there for him in those final days meant a lot to me and my family. After Uncle Bill passed, I never took the time to properly thank her."

"And now you feel you owe it to her family to find her killer."

"When I saw her laying on the beach, I couldn't believe it. It's been eating me alive ever since."

A rhythmic tone sounded from the direction of his desk. Seeward wheeled his chair over and picked up his phone. His eyes widened as he turned his back on his partner.

Hearing of the kindness exhibited by Janie Ballantine stirred a desire in Jan to reconsider her feelings toward the suggestion made by her father. If she could find Papalos and get him alone for one minute, people she knew, and some she didn't, would surely appreciate the great service she had done. Even if she was found out and her career was destroyed.

Seeward brought his chair back to her desk and leaned forward. "It's confirmed, Jan," he whispered. "Rittenhouse ordered Papalos to kill Janie Ballantine."

Jan's heart rate doubled. "We have to find him. Today."

"That's going to be a problem. The answers we received concerning his whereabouts weren't a dodge. No one close to Rittenhouse has seen him since the trial ended."

"Dammit! Well, we'll put out a bulletin saying he's wanted for questioning in a murder case. With every cop in the state looking for him, someone's bound to spot him."

"Don asked us not to do that."

"Why?"

"He said their man on the inside would keep trying to come up with the information."

Stephen Burdick

"I realize Papalos may have left the country by now, but that's taking a huge risk. Your friend is comfortable with that idea?"

"If he wasn't he wouldn't have suggested it."

"Okay, but we're not going to wait too long."

Seeward nodded.

Jan watched him as he slowly rolled his chair back to his desk.

CHAPTER 19

Jan gazed at a sky filled with angry gray clouds on her ride to work the next morning. A perfect illustration of her mood after learning Eddie Papalos was nowhere to be found, the likelihood of his being in the wind most probable.

Ten minutes later, when she walked into the homicide office, she was surprised to be greeted by her lieutenant. Unexpected, but not unusual. He was not good at hiding his feelings. His solemn demeanor and silence made obvious the notion he was about to deliver some very bad news. Several detectives already at their desks glanced up at her with uneasy eyes. The lieutenant motioned her to follow him.

Glancing at her partner's empty desk, Jan anticipated having to endure another ass-chewing after giving him an update. Like her and Seeward, he'd endured frustration far too long.

Once inside his office, the lieutenant closed the door behind her.

"Have a seat."

Jan felt her stomach tighten as she sat down.

The lieutenant rounded his desk and eased into his high-backed leather chair, pausing a moment. He stared at some papers before sitting back and folding his hands over his stomach. Then he raised his eyes.

"A situation has developed, and I need some answers from you," he said. "Some straight answers. Sergeant."

"Yes, sir."

"Do you know a Special Agent Donald Jennings with the FBI?"

"No, sir, I don't believe I do."

"You don't recall ever talking to him or meeting with him at any time?"

"No, sir. What's this all about?"

"Does Sinclair know him?"

At the mention of her partner's name, she remembered the conversations they'd had concerning Jennings. "You would have to ask him, sir."

"Don't hand me that crap, Jan. Does Sinclair know him or not?"

"He might."

The lieutenant huffed. "Yes or no, Sergeant?"

"All right!" Jan took a breath. "He once told me Jennings was a friend."

"Did Sinclair ever talk about him?"

Fear accompanied the adrenaline surging through her body. "Just to say he was a friend."

"Nothing else?"

"Lieutenant, what the hell is going on?"

The lieutenant looked away a second. "There was a shooting on a remote farm outside of Brandon last night. A guy named Eddie Papalos was shot and killed. He was part of the Colby Rittenhouse crime syndicate."

Jan relaxed and took another breath. "So, what does this have to do with Seeward?"

"Sinclair is dead, too."

Jan felt like a brick wall had fallen on her and was unable to speak. A loud, sense-shattering roar filled her ears. Now she understood. Seeward had lied about Jennings asking them not put out a state-wide bulletin.

"Jan? Jan?"

"I heard you." She lowered her head.

"I believe you told me you suspected this Papalos of somehow being involved in the murder of D. A. David Ballantine's daughter?"

"A witness saw him at Jane Ballantine's condo days before it happened. We wanted to question him, but hadn't been able to find him."

"The Feds want to know if what happened at the farm could be connected to your murder case." The lieutenant looked down at his desk. "And so do I."

Jan raised her head and choked back tears. "I don't know why Seeward was there, sir. Honestly, I don't know."

The lieutenant took a deep breath as he focused on her. "They suspect Special Agent Jennings of revealing the location of the farm to Sinclair. Did you know if such a conversation took place?"

"Seeward never said anything to me."

"You had no knowledge of his intentions?"

"No, sir."

"Is that your official statement? You had no prior knowledge of what your partner was planning to do. Is that what you want me to tell the Feds?"

"It's the truth."

"You know Sinclair will be pegged as a rogue cop on an unauthorized operation.

He'll be disgraced."

"Yes, sir."

"For the last time, Sergeant, are you saying Sinclair acted without your knowledge?"

Jan nodded.

"Then I guess that's all. I want you to go home, Jan. I know this case has been wearing on you, and in light of the circumstances..." He cleared his throat. "In fact, why don't you take a leave of absence. Check back with me in two weeks."

Jan rose and left his office. Her face glistened with tears.

The shock of her partner's death was still rippling through

her as she wandered down the hallway. Why had Seeward taken it upon himself to go after Papalos? And of more importance, why hadn't he confided in her as to knowing where Papalos would be the previous night? These and more questions she knew would never be answered would beat her down the rest of the day and for many days to come.

CHAPTER 20

The clear eastern sky glowed with pastel traces of dawn as Jan stood on the deck of the Outer Reef trawler and felt a heavy, humid breeze brush her face. With the morning free of responsibility, she looked forward to a relaxing and rewarding day. The leave of absence suggested by the lieutenant had turned out to be a wise decision. Her grief at the loss of her partner had been bordering on depression, made worse by a sense of betrayal. She'd concluded the FBI was correct in their suspicion of Don Jennings advising Seeward where Eddie Papalos could be found. For a reason known only to him, he'd chosen not to tell her. A week after his death, the reason became clear.

She'd decided to go to the grocery store one morning, and was about to get into her car when she saw an unaddressed envelope pinned under the windshield wiper. Removing the note inside, she knew from the handwriting who had written the message.

Jan,

I'm sorry things turned out the way they did. You and I both know we were never going to get Papalos, and I just couldn't let that happen. I purposely left you in the dark about everything J. had told me. I decided to go alone because I knew you would be against the idea. And if my attempt was unsuccessful, only my career would be destroyed. You taught me a lot, partner, and I wanted you to know I was a better cop and a better person for it.

Seeward

She had destroyed the message soon after, and guessed it had been delivered by Seeward's friend, Don Jennings. No one else would have agreed to the unenviable task of delivering such a note, and no one else would have known the real reason her partner had gone after Papalos. Though Seeward's story about his uncle and Janie Ballantine sounded genuine, she continued to question his true purpose for confronting the Rittenhouse gunsel. Maybe not knowing was a good thing. She knew the man and the dedicated cop he had been. Nothing or no one would ever change her mind.

As predicted, they buried Seeward without honors, a disgrace in the eyes of law enforcement. Only his family and a handful of friends attended. And David Ballantine. The district attorney passed along his condolences to her and thanked her for helping to bring closure to his family, though the cost had been far too high. In his mind, Seeward Sinclair was a hero. A hero to be respected forever.

When she got home from the funeral, she had called the lieutenant and requested another week away from the job.

As Jan listened to the methodical rhythm of the trawler's engines and the bow being slapped by the dark blue waters, her thoughts returned to the deck where she stood. She paused a moment before turning to the pilot of the fishing boat christened *Serafina* and asking a question she felt was most appropriate for the early morning excursion.

"Do you think we'll catch anything out here today, Crabby?"

A snort preceded the old salt's reply. "Do it really matter, Cap'um?"

Jan smiled as she gazed out over the Gulf of Mexico to the distant horizon.

THE ORIGINAL
THIRTEEN MURDERS

CHAPTER 1

Shortly after seven a.m., Homicide Detective Sergeant Jan Larkin looked up from her computer screen. Her new partner, Detective Jenny Lester, ambled into the office and looked in no hurry to start the day. With her brown hair pulled back in a ponytail, she reminded Jan of a 1950s high school girl. Jenny maintained an air of innocence deceiving most who didn't know her. She'd told Jan she kept her trim physique by jogging and working out in the gym.

Jenny had worked in Homicide for the Clearwater Police Department, building an exemplary record during her time on the force. From Jan's perspective, she was anything but naïve. Intelligent, street smart, and an expert on the pistol range, she had no problem adapting to the procedures and nuances of the sheriff's office. At Jan's request, they were paired after the untimely death of her former partner, Seeward Sinclair, three months ago.

Jan had spent the better part of the previous hour catching up on reports from a case they'd recently solved. As she took a sip of coffee, she decided to have some fun at the new detective's expense. "Good morning, Detective. Glad you could make it."

Jenny smiled as she set down her cup of convenience store coffee. A second later, her innocent-looking blue eyes grew wide. "Oh, no! Am I late? I thought I gave myself enough time to—." Her panic vanished after she checked the time on her phone and saw the grin on Jan's face. "Oh, Sergeant. You really had me going."

Jan laughed. "Jenny, we've been partners going on three months. I don't mind if you call me Jan."

"Okay, Sarge... uh, Jan. Can I give you a hand with those reports?"

"Nope, I'm just finishing up."

"Freshen your swill?"

"That you *can* do." The veteran detective held out her mug. "Oh, by the way, we need to go over the--."

She was cut off by the day's first interruption.

Jenny grabbed the receiver of her desk phone before the second ring. "Madeira Beach. Right. And the address? Okay, I got it."

She hung up the phone and paused while gazing at her partner's empty mug.

"Back to the homestead?" Jan asked.

Jenny looked up and nodded, with noticeable sadness filling her eyes.

Jan could tell her partner was still distracted as Jenny drove them to the crime scene. Lost in another place and time.

"Is anything wrong, Jenny?"

"No." She sighed. "Well, yes. This is the second time we've been called to Madeira Beach since I joined the sheriff's office. It was such a happy place when I was growing up. At least I thought so. I never realized bad things could happen there until I became an adult." She shook her head. "I was the poster girl for naiveté."

"Like most kids."

Her poignant recollection reminded Jan of her hometown of Lithonia, Georgia. She had been blessed with a happy childhood, unaware a dark side of humanity existed. With knowledge came a reality that sometimes left her speechless.

"Here we are," Jenny said, as she steered their gray sedan into the parking lot of the Sea Garden Condominiums.

A husky deputy met them as they got out of their car. "He's out back in the dunes, Sergeant."

"Forensics get here yet, Deputy?" Jan asked.

"On the way."

"What do we know?"

"Not very much. I thought it best to wait for you. We've got the area cordoned off. Deputy Elsworth is keeping the gawkers away."

The deputy led them into the lobby and out the rear door of the condominium. An abbreviated sidewalk gave way to the loose footing of a sandy path, presenting a challenge as they trudged between sand dunes covered in sea oats and scrub brush. To the left of where the path ended, an elderly man lay on his back surrounded by four metal poles and a rectangle of barricade tape. A considerable amount of dried blood surrounded his head. The deputy lifted the tape for the detectives.

Jan knelt down for a closer look. "Nasty wound. Looks like he was hit pretty hard."

Jenny leaned forward. "It appears as though his skull has been crushed." She straightened up. "I'll go check for witnesses."

"Don't bother with the gawkers, Detective," the deputy said. "I've talked to them already."

Jenny nodded and headed back to the condominium.

Jan stood up and surveyed the immediate area. A lesson she'd learned when she was a rookie was never to leave anything to chance. The rule had served her well. She lifted the barricade tape and began the search, knowing the likelihood of finding footprints in the loose sugar sand was next to none. She'd found nothing by the time Dave Forbes from Forensics arrived. "Dave, get all the pictures you need, then we'll turn him over and look for identification."

Forbes nodded.

"Is Judy Walker out sick today?" she asked.

"She's on vacation. The boss had to threaten her to take time off."

Jan smiled.

After he'd finished, the pair laid the man on his back.

Jan searched each pocket of the man's Bermuda shorts. She found a worn brown wallet containing the victim's driver's license and confirmed his identification. He was seventy-eight. Jenny walked up as she continued to check the rest of the wallet's contents.

"No witnesses to be found, Sergeant, uh, Jan." Jenny looked down at the man. "Any idea who he is?"

"Arthur Lee Corbett from Flemington, New Jersey."

Jenny pulled a piece of paper from the pocket of her navy-blue slacks, unfolded it, and looked over the printout.

"Yep, here he is. Staying in one of the rental units at the Sea Garden. I'll go back to the manager's office and see what else she can tell us."

Jan smiled, relieved her new partner was an experienced detective. Although part of the job included her having to hold the hand of a rookie, it was a responsibility she always dreaded. She placed the wallet inside a plastic evidence bag and slipped underneath the barricade tape.

An ambulance team appeared a short time later. Once Jan had conferred with Forbes, the team loaded the man onto a stretcher and wheeled him through the sand dunes to the ambulance.

Jan took one final look around, thought about continuing her search for evidence,

then decided to go find Jenny instead.

They met as she opened the rear entrance door to the condominium.

"Jan, I spoke to the manager, and she said Corbett was a regular visitor. He and his wife have been coming here for more than ten years. His wife passed two years ago, but Corbett continued to visit out of respect for her, and because he loved the beach."

Jan felt a twinge of sympathy for Arthur Lee Corbett, a sentiment she experienced from time to time even after twelve years in homicide. Some cases were like that. At this stage of her career, though, attempting to resist the feeling took too much out of her.

CHAPTER 2

The room inside Jerry Scanlon's studio apartment was bathed in darkness except for slices of light peeking through the holes in the worn beige curtains. The alarm clock sounded at exactly seven-thirty a.m., but he'd been awake for hours. As a teenager, he'd suffered bouts of insomnia after an eventful evening. Little had changed in the years that followed. He quieted the bell and closed his eyes.

After a few minutes, he sat up and shifted his legs to the floor. Caution was necessary to gauge his next move, especially after lying in bed for hours. His bad leg could give out at any moment. Slow to rise, he waited for signs of weakness. As so often happened first thing in the morning, a powerful urge arose inside him. Abetted by last night's celebratory beers. "I've got to get to the toilet before I break the seal," he muttered.

Halfway to the bathroom, a sharp pain tore through his left leg and he crashed to the linoleum floor. "God damn you, you son-of-a-bitch!" He hated the drunken tourist responsible for the automobile accident which left him a cripple and ended a brilliant college football career. That the man died was of little consequence to him.

The agony intensified as he rolled onto his side. He cursed again when he felt the warmth and caught a whiff of urine. As it seeped through his undershorts, he gritted his teeth and forced himself to his feet. A watery trail marked his path as he hobbled to the bathroom.

The plastic bottle he snatched from the medicine cabinet opened with little effort, and he shook three Vicodin tablets into his hand. Tossing them into his mouth, followed by a handful of water, he squeezed his eyes shut and prayed for relief. Painful moments passed before he felt the onset of that relief. He took a deep breath and slid out of his damp undershorts. Several minutes in the shower was all he needed.

He didn't bother to dry off and moved in halted steps, cursing his way across his apartment until he finally reached the dusty kitchenette. The counter helped support him and he grabbed the jar of instant coffee. He flipped his mug right-side up, added a large tablespoon and a little extra along with water and placed it in the microwave. A full ninety seconds would do the trick.

Thoughts of the previous night filled his head. He breathed deep. The tide had rolled evenly onto the shore then hissed in retreat, ushered in by the wisp of a salt-laden breeze. The moon hadn't risen yet when he'd met the old man. Darkness hid his face as well as his intentions. So scripted and simple was the attack, it almost quelled the excitement he'd anticipated. He'd been prepared for the old man to put up a fight or cry out or even try to get away. A weak attempt to land a punch and a muffled grunt was all he heard before the man dropped to the sand. So unlike the little girl in Indian Rocks Beach who had kicked him and tried to scream before he broke her neck. An infuriating and electrifying episode, but exciting nonetheless.

His next target was closer to his home, so he would have to be very careful. But then he was always careful. Vigilance drilled into him by tyrannical parents.

He raised his head when the timer bell sounded, pulled the steaming mug from inside the microwave, and blew across the top. A small sip followed by another encouraged him to take his liquid breakfast outside on the patio. He gazed at the shiny patch of urine on the floor. Mopping it up could wait.

In no hurry as he made his way across the room, his confidence improved. When he reached his dresser, he eased into a pair of gray jogging shorts. The pain from his crippled leg disappeared once he slid into the mahogany beach chair in front of his apartment. A warm morning and a healthy pull of coffee helped prepare him for his workday.

CHAPTER 3

Jan reviewed her notes and glanced at her partner from time to time. Jenny appeared to be lost in thought. Jan guessed it was Jenny's way of piecing together theories for their case. Or maybe there was something about the crime scene that reminded her of another case.

She understood cops sometimes lost sight of the tragedy and its effect on the victim's family when pursuing a killer. But every once in a while, the face of a victim would creep inside a cop's head and remind them of how unfair life could be. In this case, Arthur Lee Corbett, a widower enjoying what remained of his winter years and the simple pleasure of visiting a place he loved. Now, he would go home, never to return to Florida. The finality of that irreversible fact might be the weight on her partner's shoulders. Jan had been struggling with an unpleasant notion as well.

"Jan, I have some questions I'd like to run by you."

"Okay, but are you all right?"

"Sure. Why wouldn't I be?"

"At times, you looked like something was on your mind."

"Oh." Jenny sighed. "Arthur Corbett. He sort of resembles a man in my neighborhood when I was growing up. He was so nice. He and his wife would give me extra candy at Halloween. Anything like that ever happen to you?"

"Lately I've been thinking a lot about Seeward."

"Seeward Sinclair, your partner?"

"He used to make these goofy faces when he was going over his notes. Like he was acting out every line. Then he'd get really serious and look at me. But he wouldn't say anything." Jan smiled. "He was one of a kind."

Jenny felt uneasiness blaze a path inside her. "I didn't mean to be nosey."

"It's not a problem."

Jenny's eyes widened. "I'm sitting at his desk, aren't I?"

"Don't worry. You don't look anything like him."

Jenny laughed before covering her mouth. "Jan, I'm sorry." She paused to lower her hand. "Was he really working on his own that night in Brandon?"

"The case was complicated. And the longer it took us to catch Eddie Papalos, the more our frustration grew."

"I don't believe it, anyway."

"Don't believe what?"

"That Detective Sinclair was a rogue cop. It's unfair to slap that label on someone just because his partner isn't with him."

"Is that what you heard? That I wasn't with him?"

"I heard both of you knew where Papalos would be, and you sent Sinclair to get him. But as far as I'm concerned, we do what has to be done to serve justice."

"Within the law, you mean."

"Of course."

Jan studied her partner. "I believe communication is essential. Don't you, Detective Lester?"

"Yes, I do."

"I'm glad you agree. Now, let's do some communicating about our current case."

Jenny glanced at her notes. "I don't think this was a robbery. I mean, we found his wallet intact. Money, credit cards, identification, nothing was missing."

Jan nodded.

"Why was he targeted? People living in his condo said he

was quiet, easy to like, and polite. Jan, I've gone over his personal history, and there's nothing there to raise a red flag. I mean, this guy was the chief financial officer for the Garden State Agricultural Commission. He'd won awards for efficiency and performance. He was an employee of the year three times and never had a bad mark against him in his personnel file. And there were never any improprieties or questions about his audits."

"Maybe he crossed the wrong person."

"Jan, Corbett was a decorated war hero. He received a Silver Star, a Bronze Star,

and the Purple Heart for serving in Viet Nam. I mean, this guy fought in the Ia Drang Valley."

"The Ia Drang Valley?"

"Some of the fiercest and most deadly battles were fought there, yet this guy gets taken down without a struggle? I mean, I know he was nearly eighty years old, but that doesn't make sense to me. I'm thinking the killer was someone he knew. Or, at least, someone he felt didn't pose a threat." Jenny paused. "Why are you smiling like that?"

"I'm waiting for you to breathe."

A blush warmed the new detective's face.

"Jenny, you've done well, and I agree with you." Jan decided to take her protégé in a different direction. "Did you notice those peculiar lines in the sand? The ones away from the body?"

"Yes. Well, I mean, I did after Dave Forbes pointed them out."

"What do you think caused them?"

"At first, I thought someone might have been dragging something, like maybe a folded-up umbrella that was too heavy. Or a kid's beach toy. But the lines weren't continuous. And the more I thought about the width and the spacing, it almost looked like someone was limping."

"How far did you follow the trail?"

"About twenty yards or more."

"And that's where it stopped?"

"Like he paused or something. Then the trail picked up again, only not so deep. Then it disappeared...kind of. If that was still him, I mean."

"Did you discover any actual footprints?"

"Well, not exactly. Most often all you get are partials in sugar sand. And you already know that because you're smiling again."

"Jenny, I have one last question."

"What is it?"

"How do you know the killer is a 'he'?"

CHAPTER 4

In the glow of the half moon, small waves rose and fell, rushing to the shore to deposit their serpentine foam before mounting a retreat. The floodlights at the rear of the hotel spread over the sand, but left the row of wooden beach chairs near the shoreline in the shadows. Jerry Scanlon dug his toes into the sand and enjoyed its coolness as he rested on one of the chairs. Periodic winds sailed in and made it easy for him to conclude the temperature was somewhere in the upper sixties—knowledge only someone born and raised in Florida would possess. The night walkers, those who preferred the quiet and sometimes eerie seashore after dark, became fewer as the evening grew later.

His manner was polite as he greeted all who passed, even taking a moment to assist a disoriented couple unable to find their motel. As far as anyone knew, he was someone who appreciated the beach at night. One who found serenity to be the best way to work out a problem. Someone with a broken heart and an unspoken desire to find closure.

As he had done several times before, he glanced over his shoulder in anticipation. His patience was rewarded when he saw a woman approaching. Lost in the wonder of a star-strewn sky, the woman didn't notice him right away. "Good evening," he said. "Beautiful night, isn't it?"

Startled, she recoiled a half step, didn't answer, then walked a wide path around him.

"You don't remember me, do you? Your friend, Vickie, introduced us. She was part of the wedding party staying at the Lost Treasure motel."

The young woman stopped, turned, and faced him. "I'm sorry," she said. "I didn't recognize you in the dark. You're the guy who cleans the pools, right? Jerry Scanlon, isn't it?"

"And you're Elaine Fuller." When first meeting her, she'd reminded him of a girl he'd met in college. A girl who'd toyed with him before running back home to her boyfriend in New England.

"What are you doing out here?"

"Well, my girlfriend and I just broke up. I came out here to... You know."

"Jerry, I'm so sorry." She stepped closer to him.

"It's okay. I just needed to clear my head. And the beach at night is so peaceful."

"Every night has been gorgeous. I just love it here."

He looked down and kicked the sand, his resentment building. "It's getting late. I guess I'd better be going."

"Jerry, are you going to be all right?"

"I'll get over it. I always do."

"Well, it was nice to see you again."

She turned to leave, not noticing he'd gotten to his feet. Scanlon clamped his arms around her and slapped his hand over her mouth. He forced her body against his as he rammed the hunting knife under her ribcage. The blade went in easier than he'd anticipated.

She flailed the air in an attempt to break free. A second thrust of the knife brought a muffled scream. She lowered her arms to her sides.

Scanlon looked around to make sure they were alone before laying her limp body face down in the sand. He wiped the knife clean on her dark blue hoodie, donned his flip-flops, and walked south along the water's edge. Keeping the lights of the

Lost Treasure motel in sight, he needed to get to his truck as soon as possible. As the flood of adrenaline inside him waned, his breathing returned to normal. Three steps later a soreness in his left leg began to grow.

"Not now! Not now!" he whispered, and groaned.

He left the water's edge and struggled through the loose sand, the pain in his leg growing stronger. A three-foot-high concrete wall outlined the motel parking lot where he'd left his truck. He pulled up ten yards away from the wall. The pain in his leg was unbearable. He knew he must keep moving and scanned the immediate area to make certain he hadn't been seen. Shoving his hand into his pocket, he removed a pill bottle, shook out three Vicodin, and tossed them into his mouth. Hard to swallow, he gritted his teeth and waited. Another cool breeze sailing in from the Gulf accompanied a sense of relief. Scanlon let go a long and heavy sigh and hobbled to the wall. The pain lessened and convinced him to place both hands under his left knee and lift his troublesome leg over the wall. Once he'd swung his right leg over, he paused to steady himself and catch his breath. "I will make it," he whispered. "Unlike you, Elaine Fuller, I will make it." Taking a last look around, he heard only the subdued crashing of the surf. He slowly stood up and limped toward his truck.

The ceiling in Scanlon's bedroom was cracked and peeling and in need of repair in the worst way. He'd noticed it many times and reported it to his landlord, but the problem had not been addressed. For some reason, the surface was most annoying today. Maybe the return of pain in his leg brought on his foul mood. by. Or the contempt he felt for his ramshackle surroundings. Whatever the cause, he was tired of the persistent misery and the effort it took to survive.

The effects of his latest encounter were evident, so he decided to stay home.

After all, the world wouldn't come to an end without the presence of the crippled pool cleaner. His reliable reputation would keep him in good standing with his clients when he called them to say he was sick. And they would accept his promise to come by in a day or two. Anyway, it was better he didn't risk going outside. One of his clients lived in the vicinity of the Four Winds Resort. The last thing he wanted or needed was an accidental encounter with the law.

He sighed and closed his eyes right before a searing pain ripped a path through his leg. He cried out and cursed his misfortune as he had done so many times before. And as he had also done so many times before, he considered putting an end to his suffering. Forever. But a personal vow made years ago quickly dispelled the thought. He waited for the pain to subside. He would persevere until the vow was fulfilled.

CHAPTER 5

Jan jumped awake, choking on the acrid odor lingering and burning her throat. Sleep had eluded her for most of the night. When it finally arrived, her dreams were disturbing and unforgiving. Occasional dreams which began a decade ago, two years after she became a detective. They occurred more often during a difficult case. She tried to shake the heaviness from her head. She gazed at the clock on the nightstand beside her bed. The glowing green numbers indicated the alarm she despised would sound in two hours. Not close to coherent, she pondered the significance of the dreams, the second one the most memorable.

In the first dream, she leaned against a split-rail fence that surrounded a farmhouse. She watched a young man wielding an automatic creep toward the front of the house. When he stopped and brought the automatic to shoulder level with both hands, he yelled something she couldn't understand. The front door flew open, and a second man rushed out with his automatic raised. The sound of gunfire shattered the countryside and echoed over a meadow beyond as both men dropped to the ground.

Spurred on by an uneasy feeling that, somehow, she knew the first shooter, she started to run to him. But her legs felt heavy and slowed her down. Horror swept over her when she finally reached the man and discovered he was her partner,

Seeward Sinclair. He begged her to help him, but she couldn't move, and stood helplessly by as he died.

In the second dream, she stood beside a casket in a funeral home surrounded by strangers. She didn't know why she was there, but when she looked into the casket, she saw her father lying underwater, and a strong odor of chlorine filled her nostrils.

Her father had died twenty-three years ago, and she had seen him in his casket. But he hadn't drowned. Skin cancer from too many days in the sun had claimed him. And what did the smell of chlorine have to do with anything?

Jan kicked her feet to the floor, plodded across her darkened bedroom, and filled the bathroom sink with water. The first splash of water on her face wasn't helpful. During the second dousing, she inadvertently inhaled which provoked a violent coughing binge. She took a deep breath and gazed in the mirror. The tired cop she'd seen too many times stared back with droplets of water trickling down her face. A cop who had seen too much for too long. A cop on the verge of hanging up her gun. "Once this case is over, I'm going to get a life."

Leaving the bathroom, she collapsed on the sofa and thought of making coffee, but lost the desire to move again and closed her eyes. The alarm sounded, but she didn't care.

CHAPTER 6

Jan trudged into the office and headed straight for the coffee station.

"Good morning, Jan. I was starting to wonder where you were," Jenny said.

"I had a rough night. Any new developments?" Jan passed by her without waiting for an answer.

"No, but I was thinking we might--" Jenny glared at the ringing phone on her desk. Calls always seemed to come at every inappropriate moment. She grabbed the receiver. "What's the address? Okay, got it." She wheeled her chair around. "Jan, some woman in Seminole just shot her husband."

"I wish someone would shoot me," Jan mumbled as she filled her mug. She blew across the top of it then took a sip of steamy coffee. "Okay, let's go."

Jenny hesitated and stared at her. "Would you like me to handle it? You don't look so good."

"Listen, Detective, the day I can't do my job is the day I quit."

The pair arrived in Seminole to find there was no mystery to be uncovered at the quaint blue house nestled among the many oak trees. A man lay dead on the living room floor, shot three times in the chest. A woman sat crying in a chair nearby.

The deputy to arrive first on the scene had confiscated the murder weapon, a .38 caliber revolver, and stood guard over the woman until they arrived.

As Jenny questioned her, the woman called her husband a philanderer along with other, more colorful names. Once her emotional tirade ended, she admitted to killing him. She was handcuffed, advised of her rights, and taken away.

Neighbors told the detectives the couple argued often, but they'd never seen any acts of violence on the part of either—until now. Once their investigation was completed, the detectives headed back to the office.

An uneasy feeling had shadowed Jenny since the morning began. Now it pushed her to probe further into the personal life of Sergeant Jan Larkin. If she would be allowed inside. "Jan, I have no right to ask, but is there something about the killing of the old man in Madeira Beach that's bothering you? Personally, I mean?"

"Mind your own business, Detective!" Jan barked. A moment later she sighed. "Jenny, I'm sorry. I'm just tired. I had two nightmares between not sleeping last night, and one of them really has me perturbed."

Jan sensed her partner's reluctance to inquire as to the nature of her dreams and volunteered an explanation. She recounted the shooting, and how she felt when Seeward had called her name before he'd died. The scene continued to haunt her because she'd been unable to help him. And as bad as that had been, she'd found the second dream much more puzzling and distressing.

"I remember feeling confused. I couldn't figure out why so many strangers had come to Dad's funeral. Only my family and some of his friends came to the actual service. And his being underwater along with the strong odor of chlorine made no sense at all."

"Did your father drown?" Jenny asked.

"He died from skin cancer. He spent most days in the peach orchard from sunup to sundown."

"Hmm."

"What are you thinking?"

"I was just thinking about the significance of him being submerged. I mean, I've had dreams about people I didn't know and places I've never been, and I can't tell you why I did. But your father was nowhere near water at the time of his death. I find that strange."

Jan nodded, equally curious as to the subliminal meaning of both dreams.

CHAPTER 7

The clamor of sun worshipers leaving Pass-A-Grille Beach mingled with the scent of seaweed and coconut oil that rode on the breezes as Jerry Scanlon sat in front of his apartment. Seagulls screeched overhead, and the sun prepared to dive behind a large, gray-black thundercloud out over the Gulf of Mexico. He felt much better after a day off from work. The pills and half-dozen beers had done away with his pain and the possibility of any other discomfort which might have arisen.

Although he allowed thoughts of his latest achievement to slip in and out of his mind, his primary focus was on the selection of the next unsuspecting target. An inner voice suggested the objective should be at least twenty miles or more away from the beach. Oldsmar or Safety Harbor would be prime alternatives to serve his purpose. With no definite pattern to his plan, law enforcement agencies would be oblivious to the possibility of a solitary hunter. He grinned. He preferred the title of hunter over the more popular label—serial killer. Many innocent people would fall prey to the good-natured pool maintenance man before the cops drew any kind of connection. And that would give him plenty of time to achieve his goal.

His grin grew into a smile as he took a pull of beer and toasted yet another twilight auburn sky.

CHAPTER 8

Scanlon glanced at his watch as he rang the doorbell. He was thirty minutes late for his appointment, and though the hour was nearing noon, he knew Tony and Emma Gerard wouldn't mind. They were people of a casual nature. Retirees who'd worked hard to improve every aspect of their life together so they might enjoy their twilight years. The neighborhood was quiet, and he smiled to himself until Mrs. Gerard opened the door.

"Hello, Jerry. How are you feeling?"

"Fine, Mrs. Gerard. I'm sorry I couldn't make it yesterday. My leg was bothering me."

"Oh, you poor dear."

"Well, I'd better get right to it. I've got a lot of catching up to do."

"I was about to start lunch. Would you care to join us?"

"Oh, I don't want to put you to all that trouble."

"It's no trouble. We'd love to have you."

"Well, okay. I could use a break." Scanlon offered his most charming smile.

"It's nothing special. Sliced turkey sandwiches and cole-slaw."

"Sounds delicious. Thank you."

Scanlon walked around the side of the house and entered through the door to the screen encasement protecting the pool.

As he set foot on the pool deck, he noticed Mr.
Gerard sitting at a glass-topped aluminum table with a book
in his hand. He cleared his throat.

"Good morning, Mr. Gerard."

Gerard half-turned and looked over the top of his glasses.
"Jerry! Are you feeling better today?"

"Much better, thank you. My leg makes life difficult at
times."

"That's too bad."

"Mrs. Gerard invited me to stay for lunch."

"Good deal. That will give us plenty of time to talk football.
I don't get the opportunity often."

"I'd like that, sir."

"Please, have a seat." Gerard laid down his book.

Scanlon pulled out a chair and sat down.

Gerard leaned to his left and strained a look through the
sliding glass door. "She's still in the kitchen." He turned back to
Scanlon. "Now, as I recall, you follow college football, is that
right?"

"Yes, sir. I like pro football, but college teams don't have
that many players who can cut it in the show."

"And why does that interest you?"

"Because college kids make more mistakes. It can be very
annoying at times or very exciting."

"Who's your favorite team?"

"The USF Bulls."

"Of course. I forgot you played for them."

"Actually, I pull for all the Florida teams."

"Any players you think will make a splash in the pros?"

"Well, there's this kid at UCF, a defensive back, who looks
to be—"

"It's ready!" Mrs. Gerard sang out as she breezed up to the
table. She set two plates in front of them. "I'll be right back
with the iced tea. Is that okay with you, Jerry?"

"Certainly, Mrs. Gerard."

"So much for football," Gerard said. He grinned. "Prepare yourself for a barrage of questions about your social life."

Scanlon smiled. He would oblige his hosts with menial conversation, taking care to remain polite throughout the meal. Keep the Gerards oblivious to what lay in store for them. Both were former educators who had polluted his home state with their northern attitudes. And they were intelligent people. They would notice the least little change in his behavior.

Mrs. Gerard returned with their drinks and her sandwich. True to her husband's words, she peppered Scanlon with questions about his lack of lady friends.

Gerard cut glances at him every so often and smiled.

"And this interior decorator just announced one day it was over between you?" Mrs. Gerard said.

"It was pretty obvious, Mrs. Gerard. She admitted she was looking for someone different than me."

"Different? What does that mean?"

"She never came right out and said it, but I think my handicap might have been the reason."

"But you're a handsome man, Jerry. And you're polite and you care about people."

Scanlon shrugged.

"Different strokes for different folks," Gerard said through a mouthful.

Emma huffed. "What about the administrative assistant?"

"Well..." Scanlon finished the last of his coleslaw. "...she said I didn't make enough money."

"Jerry, that's terrible. A bitch like that should be—"

"Now, darling," Gerard said. "I think you've quizzed Jerry enough about his personal life."

Scanlon smiled. "It's okay, Mrs. Gerard, I got over them. I always do. Now, if you both will excuse me, I need to get to work. Thanks again for lunch."

"You're welcome, Jerry," Gerard said and picked up his book.

Mrs. Gerard began to clear the table.

Scanlon walked over to the canvas tool bag he'd set by the pool, knelt down, and pulled out a comparator tube. He pretended to take a sample of water to measure the pH balance before glancing over his shoulder. Mrs. Gerard had picked up their plates and glasses and was carrying them into the house. Mr. Gerard was engrossed in his book.

Scanlon returned the tube to the bag and removed a two-pound drilling hammer. Worn out sneakers muffled his approach. He stood over Gerard a second before winding up and bashing the gentleman in the back of the head. The blow sent Gerard sprawling across the table and shattered the glass before he hit the deck. Without hesitation, Scanlon hurried to the wall beside the open sliding glass door, hidden from view by a drawn velvet curtain. Mrs. Gerard appeared in the breach and shrieked when she saw her fallen husband.

Scanlon waited until she ran to his side then crept up behind her. The second execution was a gift to be treasured. As he was about to follow through, Mrs. Gerard turned around. Terror filled her eyes a heartbeat before he drove the hammer into her forehead. A smile of satisfaction curled the corners of his mouth. His eyes never left her as he knelt down and wiped the blood from the face of the hammer on her sunny yellow apron. He picked up the canvas bag, dropped the hammer inside, and took a moment to savor his accomplishment. A low moan wiped the smile from his face. He reached for a hunting knife inside the bag and walked over to where she lay over her husband's outstretched legs. Mrs. Gerard moaned again.

A swift and clean slicing of both their throats guaranteed the genteel couple would never see their family again. Scanlon paused to make certain he'd done a thorough job. Confident he'd succeeded, he picked up the bag and exited through the screen door.

Tossing his tool bag into the rear of his truck, Scanlon heaved deep breaths, and drew upon the adrenaline fueling his rage. The memory of the attack still vivid in his mind, he climbed inside his truck and backed out of the driveway bound for his next appointment in Largo.

CHAPTER 9

Jan stood three feet from the large white board, aptly named the clue board, with her left arm across her stomach, right arm pointed upwards to her face, hand pulling on her chin. Like a statue frozen in time, her steadfast focus and intensity sustained a determined effort not to give in to the unsolvable puzzle until she found an answer.

Before they returned to the office, she and Jenny had stopped off in Madeira Beach to go over the crime scene where Arthur Lee Corbett had been murdered. They'd hoped to discover some evidence they may have overlooked during their previous visit. They came away with nothing.

Jenny sighed and pushed away from her desk. She leaned back in the chair and stared at the ceiling. The afternoon was fading. She rose and joined her partner at the clue board.

"Jan, I'm not getting anywhere. Why don't we call it a day?"

Oblivious, her partner didn't answer.

"Jan?"

As if slapped by an unseen hand, the veteran detective jumped. "What! Oh. Jenny. I was just trying to figure out why... What did you say?"

"The Corbett case. I've gone over my notes three times."

"Yeah, I know what you mean. After what you told me about him being a veteran,

I still can't figure out how he was taken out so easily and

why no one saw or heard anything."

"I think it's time we head for home. We can take it up again tomorrow...if that's okay with you."

"Yeah, I suppose so." Jan looked back at the clue board. "I just want to go over this one more time."

"My friend Debbie and I are going out tonight for some beers and fun. Would you like to come with us?"

"Thanks, Jenny, but I'm going to turn in early."

"Okay, but know you're always welcome."

The young detective picked up her belongings and left.

In truth, Jan *was* tired. Not from fatigue so much as aggravation. There was not a hint of evidence to be found, and that always drove her crazy. If they kept coming up empty as they continued with their investigation, the case would eventually go cold. She didn't like to lose.

CHAPTER 10

Nothing was going right as Jan addressed the traffic with a barrage of colorful comments on her way home. In the middle of one long and drawn-out tirade, the image of her partner floated into her mind.

During their short amount of time together, she had come to appreciate Jenny, a consummate professional in every way. In the past, Jan wouldn't have thought twice about accepting an offer to go out for a beer. But she'd made a promise to herself after Seeward was killed. Never again would she get that close to another detective. Losing him had devastated her. Losing another partner would destroy her.

Of late, her favorite watering hole had become the Spinnaker Bar and Grill. She'd changed her mind about turning in early and decided a couple of beers would do her good. At the sight of the humble Treasure Island establishment, she felt better as she entered the parking lot.

The Spinnaker was more crowded than usual, due primarily to the influx of winter visitors. Instead of waiting for a booth, Jan headed straight for the bar. She slid into a vacant chair between two men and tried to catch the eye of Hank the bartender. Glancing to her left, she spied an old friend sitting alone at the end of the bar. She left the chair and meandered through the crowd to where he was seated. The saltwater relic didn't see her as she slipped up beside him.

"New in town, sailor?" she said.

After a quick a snort, the ancient mariner turned and smiled. "Buy ya a beer, Cap'um?"

They both laughed.

The man seated next to Crabby Phillips rose and offered Jan his chair.

"Hank, a beer for my friend!" Crabby bellowed.

"Thanks, Crabby."

"Jan, ya look tired. Ya got another tough one?"

"Yeah, and it looks like I'm staring at a dead end."

Hank the bartender appeared with a mug of beer and set it in front of her.

"And two shots of whiskey when you get a chance," she said.

"Comin' right up," Hank said with a smile.

Jan was about to enjoy a healthy pull from her frosty mug when Hank came back with the shots. "That was quick."

"We aim to please," he said.

She slid one of the shots over to Crabby. They raised their glasses and toasted their friendship. The noise level was rising, but she felt right at home.

Crabby downed the last of his brew. "How's the kid?"

"She's doing a great job. She makes my life so much easier since... since she came on board."

"You oughter bring 'er in sometime. I'd likes ta meet, uh, what's 'er name?"

"Jenny." Jan took a masterful drink of beer.

Crabby glanced sideways at her. "Speakin' of yer life, how's it goin'?"

"My life? Well, Crabby, my life never really changes." She signaled Hank for two more beers. "You know, kind of like yours."

The old salt offered a solemn expression.

Hank returned with two more beers and picked up their empty mugs.

Crabby grabbed one of the frosty brews, but didn't take a drink. "I likes muh life, Jan. But I don't think ya like yers."

"Of course I do. I love being a cop."

The woman seated on her right turned to Jan wearing a peculiar expression at the mention of the word "cop."

"I ain't talkin' 'bout that. I'm talkin' 'bout *yer* life. Ain't there some fella yer keepin' comp'ny with or anythin'?"

Jan laughed as she spilled some of her beer on the counter. "You're the only man in my life. What could be better?"

Crabby scowled. "Aw, Jan, I ain't talkin' 'bout that kinda thing."

"I know, but dating a cop isn't easy. It's much too complicated for most men. It's too complicated for most people, actually. My hours are weird, and when I get caught up in a case, I don't give a man the attention he wants or deserves. I'm exhausted at the end of the day. Every day, it feels like lately. And it never stops. Believe me. I've been a detective for a long time."

They drank a little longer and listened to the crowd.

"It ain't none o' my bidness, Jan, but ya don't need ta be spendin' yer time in here with me. Yer a good lookin' woman. Ya should be enjoyin' yerself with somebuddy else."

Jan's mouth dropped open. "Why, you loveable old seadog." She threw her arms around him and kissed him on the cheek.

He pushed her away and swabbed his face with his hand. "Now stop that!"

She laughed and kissed him again.

CHAPTER 11

On a quiet Thursday afternoon, Scanlon stood by the screen door and watched the young blonde from New York slide through the water with ease. The granddaughter of his clients, the McConnells, was enjoying her time alone in the pool while her grandmother and grandfather were away. The McConnell's adored their granddaughter and had told him a great deal about her.

Her black string bikini clung to her well-defined, tanned body, and her long blonde hair flowed freely with each unhurried stroke. For a moment he was hypnotized by her beauty, part of him desirous and sorry for what he was about to do. When she stopped in the shallow end and wiped the water from her face, an impulsive darkness overwhelmed him. Diluted the weakness and hardened his heart.

"Excuse me. I'm here to clean the pool," he said.

The woman flinched, then giggled after she whirled around. Sparkling blue eyes highlighted a dazzling smile. She seemed to recognize him. "Guess I'd better get out of your way, then."

When she stepped out of the pool, streams of water flowed down the curves of her body. She picked up a pink beach towel from the chaise lounge a few feet away to dry herself.

Scanlon placed his tool bag on the deck. Instead of beginning his work, he glanced around the yard. The privacy fence was sturdy and a guarantee of solitude. The woman was facing away from him, and had no idea he had moved to within two feet of her. *You Yankee girls all alike*, he thought. *Play with a fellow's emotions, then dump him without a second thought.* His arms were extended out, and his hands were about to encircle her neck when she surprised him by turning around.

Both of them froze.

Her reaction was quicker than his, and she drove her right fist into his mouth. The punch was solid and knocked his head back. She turned to run, but he recovered and clamped his calloused hands around her throat. She elbowed him in the stomach and fought to pull his hands away as they grappled. He forced her down, slammed her face into the deck, but she continued to squirm and flail wildly with him on top of her. A handful of her blonde hair made it easy for him to smash her face into the concrete again. He latched onto her throat with his vise-like grip and squeezed tighter and harder. In a matter of seconds, she lay still.

His hands were still locked around her throat as he heaved deep breaths and tasted blood. A split lip was a small price to pay for this triumph. He loosened his grasp, straightened up, and wiped his mouth with two fingers. Then he grinned, exhilarated.

He stared at the dead girl one last time, got to his feet, and picked up his tool bag. His escape was halted by a crunching sound. The powdered remains of a pain pill lay under his boot. His prescription bottle and a good many pills had scattered around the girl's body. Elation abandoned him as he scooped up the bottle and threw the pills inside.

Next time, he would leave the damn thing in his truck.

On the way back to his apartment, Scanlon tasted blood once more. The idea of taking a long-needed vacation entered his mind. His good friend Charles Lyon owned a lakeside cabin outside of Floral City, about seventy miles north of Tampa. The cabin would be the perfect place to hide out until things quieted down.

Scanlon took time to survey his neighborhood as he eased into the driveway. Seeing no one, he hurried as best he could from his truck and unlocked the front door.

The image he saw in the bathroom mirror sported a dime-sized splotch of dried blood on his chin, the drainage a result of his split lower lip. His right eye was swollen and decorated with a noticeable bruise. He couldn't recall how he'd gotten the bruise. Had he and the girl butted heads when he'd taken her down? No matter.

He cleaned and doctored himself, then sat down in a chair at his small dining table. When the time felt right, he picked up his phone.

"Yellow!"

"How you doin', Charles? It's Jeff.."

"Dude! What up?"

Charles had known him since childhood as Jeff, his middle name.

"Oh, you know, just enjoying the last few days of spring. And speaking of spring,

I was wondering if I could use your cabin in Floral City for a couple of weeks. I really need to get away."

"No problem, amigo. It's yours for as long as you like. The key is under a ceramic frog in the garden by the front door. The garden is probably overgrown by now, so you may have to dig a little."

"I'll find it. And thanks, man. I really owe you for this."

"Not a thing, dude. Just remember me when you win the lottery."

Scanlon sighed as he ended the call, happy his friend had been able to accommodate him. He could use the time to relax and heal.

One by one, he called his clients and told them there had been a death in his family, and he would get back to them in a week or so. He decided to leave as soon as he'd cleaned out his truck and packed his bags.

CHAPTER 12

The ride up U.S. 41 was tranquil compared to the speed-driven mentality of interstate highway travel. Rural Florida in the spring was a welcome change of pace from the urban rat race. Cooler temperatures ruled the days and nights, and the pastoral atmosphere hinted of life once lived in an easier time. Towns with names such as Shady Grove, Istachatta, Summerfield, and Masaryktown seemed a world away from the metropolitan sprawls of Jacksonville, Tampa, and Miami. Friendly businesses with quaint names like Deb's Back Porch Bar, Ukulele Sam's Lakefront Grill, and Tin Can Pam's Discount Groceries dotted the roadside. And the call of places like Duck Slough, Jumper Creek, and the Chinsegut Hill Recreation Area captured the attention of those with the need to spend some time in the wild.

The sign announcing his arrival in Floral City released a tired but gratifying feeling in Scanlon. He turned right onto East Orange Avenue and was immediately captivated. A magical, therapeutic quality emanated from the beautiful little community, and quelled the pain of his injuries. A short distance and another right turn found him on the shaded thoroughfare of Great Oaks Drive.

The peace and quiet of the country breathed new life into him as he rolled along the two-lane asphalt road. A left turn onto Oak Ridge Street brought the euphoria he craved and hoped he would find in retirement. A few homes here and there and trees as far as he could see were a dream come true. Most of all, the clean, fresh air was therapeutic in clearing his mind. He felt as though he'd discovered paradise.

A lazy U-turn onto Lake Shore Drive guided him to the last leg of his journey and the cabin. He recognized the entrance in the barbed-wire fence and turned left onto a driveway of two ruts worn into a continuous bed of St. Augustine grass. The rustic, two-bedroom cabin boasted a screened porch that looked toward the lake and brought a smile to his face. It sat a little more than halfway between the road and the lake in a clearing spotted with live oaks. The clearing gave way to a host of cypress trees along the water's edge. To the left side of the cabin was a sparse but constant stand of oaks. The right side was wide open to the fence that marked the property line. In the rear, a thirty-foot wooden dock surrounded by lily pads sat atop the dark waters of a small lagoon off Lake Bradley. Lashed to the dock was a fourteen-foot john boat.

Scanlon took a deep breath and got out of his truck. Stretching and taking another deep breath, he ambled toward the cabin. A blanket of weeds and grass covered the untended planters on either side of the concrete steps leading up to the front door. The ceramic frog was all but covered in the garden on his left, but, as his friend had indicated, the key lay underneath. He returned to his truck and retrieved his two suitcases.

As he placed his luggage in the bedroom closet, a pain shot through the right side of his face. An unpleasant reminder of his encounter with the girl. He went to the small kitchen sink for a glass of water and downed three Vicodins.

When the pain subsided, he went outside and pulled his truck around behind the cabin. With the necessary tasks completed, he stood with his back to the screened porch and looked out over at the lake. The sun was late in the western sky, and the symphony of amphibians and cicadas rang in a melodious crescendo. Feeling the need to get off of his feet, he entered the porch and spotted a lone wicker chair with its thick brown cushions. The chair would serve as his throne during his stay. Once seated, the onset of sleep was quick.

CHAPTER 13

Jan stood in her usual spot in front of the clue board going over the photos of the victim along with addresses and other information they'd acquired, but not giving it her full attention. She and Jenny had scoured the Arthur Lee Corbett crime scene a third time and questioned a few more residents in his condo. Their effort proved to be a waste of time. She jerked her head around when the telephone on Jenny's desk rang. Jenny cupped a yawn with her hand and glared at the irritating interruption before she picked up the receiver. "All right, what's the address?" she said. "Got it." She replaced the receiver and shook her head. "Jan, we've got another one."

Jan stared at the clue board a few more seconds. "Okay. You drive."

The ride to Seminole from their office on Ulmerton Road was short. A good thing, as both detectives were somewhat annoyed. Neither was in the mood to deal with another murder when they weren't even making progress on the Corbett case.

Forensics was well into the crime scene when they arrived. Dave Forbes met them with his usual no-nonsense report.

"Female, twenty, abrasions on her face and knees. Abrasions on her elbows, too." he said. "There appears to have been a struggle, but I don't believe it lasted long. We did find some prints, however."

"Doesn't look like he tried to rape her," Jan said. "She still has her bikini bottoms on. Any idea how she was killed?"

Forbes stared at the young woman. "With her lying face down, it's difficult to tell. From the condition of her face, though, it might be blunt force trauma. Hard to say. But she pretty much died where you see her now."

"What's that you have there, Dave?" Jenny asked.

Forbes held up a plastic evidence bag containing a small amount of white powder. "Found it over there." He pointed to a small plastic evidence sign. "I'm not sure what it is. I could hazard a guess, but I'd rather wait until I can run some tests."

Jan and Jenny walked over to the body, knelt down, and turned the woman over. Though her face was bloodied, her eyes were still open. Fear was her final expression.

"Dave might be right about the way she died, Jenny," Jan said. "It does appear her face was smashed into the pool deck."

A deputy pushed open the sliding glass door to the house.

"Sergeant Larkin, the grandparents, Martha and James McConnell, are in here."

The detectives stood up and walked into the house. They found the McConnells seated on a sofa, sobbing.

Jenny walked to the front door to check for forced entry while Jan addressed them.

"I'm Detective Sergeant Larkin, and I'm sorry for your loss. I know this isn't a good time, but I'd like to ask you some questions."

Mrs. McConnell looked up and dabbed a tissue on her tear-stained face. Mr. McConnell continued to hang his head.

"The woman by the pool, is she related to you?"

"Our granddaughter," Mrs. McConnell said and sniffed. "Amanda Lynn McConnell. She lives in White Plains, New York."

"Did she visit you often?"

"Whenever she could. Even as a child, she loved coming to see us. And we loved having her."

"I take it you and Mr. McConnell were away for part of the day."

Mrs. McConnell nodded. "We were at the senior center for our weekly bridge game. When we came home, we found her...lying out there."

Mr. McConnell suddenly broke down. "I'm sorry. I just can't do this." He rose and disappeared down the hall.

Mrs. McConnell watched her husband until he was gone. "Amanda was his favorite. We love all our grandchildren, but she was his favorite from the time she could walk. And she loved her Paw-Paw." She dropped her head and began to sob.

Jan gave her a moment. "I know this is difficult for you, Mrs. McConnell, but are you certain the house was locked?"

"We told Amanda to always lock the doors when she was alone."

"So, there's no way anyone could have gotten inside without her knowing?"

"She was always good about locking up."

"Do you have any idea of who might have done this?"

"I can't think of anyone."

"Did Amanda ever mention having a problem with anyone while she was visiting you?"

"No. She never went anywhere alone. We always went out together."

"Mrs. McConnell, when my partner and I arrived, we came through the screen door to your pool. Did you open it for the deputies when they arrived?"

"No, we left it open for Jerry."

"And who is Jerry?"

"Jerry Scanlon. He cleans our pool."

Jan wrote down the name in her notepad. "Do you have a phone number for him?"

Mrs. McConnell gestured toward the kitchen. "It's in there...somewhere."

"If I could have that number."

"Oh, yes. Of course."

The brokenhearted grandmother rose and headed to the kitchen, to the refrigerator door covered with post-it notes and children's crayon drawings. She slid a business card from under the *World's Greatest Grandparents* magnet and handed it to Jan.

"I guess he didn't make it," she said softly.

"Why do you say that?"

"He always locks up after he's finished. He's conscientious." Mrs. McConnell paused. "I wish he had been here. Maybe he could have stopped whoever..." She buried her face in her hands and began to cry.

"Thank you, Mrs. McConnell. And again, I'm sorry."

Jan was curious to know how Martha McConnell seemed so certain the pool man hadn't been there, but didn't push her. Maybe the screen door being unlocked was the answer. Anyone could have come through it. She was making more notes when she heard her partner call out.

"Jan, come look at this."

Jenny had returned to the pool deck and was standing by the outside of the house. As Jan approached her, she knelt down to where the house and the pool deck came together, and pushed a white tablet into an evidence bag with her pen.

"I found this partially hidden by a towel. It's a Vicodin tablet."

Jan nodded and pulled her phone from the pocket of her slacks. "Martha McConnell mentioned the name of their pool maintenance man. He was supposed to come by and clean the pool today."

After Jenny gave the newfound evidence to Dave Forbes, she returned to her partner and noticed a puzzled expression on Jan's face.

"No luck with the pool boy?" she said.

"I left a message, but when the recording came on, there was no mention of a pool service."

"Maybe it's his personal phone."

"Could be. It seems odd, though, since the number is on his business card."

"Maybe it's a one-man operation and he freelances. Or maybe he's lacking in the intelligence and personality departments."

Jan shrugged. "Would you see if you can pull up where he lives on your phone? Maybe we can catch him at home."

Jenny was successful in locating the address of Jerry Scanlon's apartment.

After the detectives finished their investigation, they headed in the direction of his St. Petersburg Beach home. Uneasiness and the knowledge the life of the pretty young visitor had ended much too soon rode with them.

CHAPTER 14

Early evening found Jan alone at her desk in the homicide office. She and Jenny had come up empty after they arrived at Jerry Scanlon's apartment. And a second attempt to phone him had failed. The onset of a headache and the prospect of another sleepless night was the primary cause of her distress. She got up and walked over to the clue board to review what little was known about the Corbett and McConnell murder cases.

Arthur Corbett, a retiree, was killed at night on the beach by a blow to the head. Amanda McConnell, a young woman visiting her grandparents, was killed during the day in suburbia, her cause of death currently unknown. The cases were very different. And too many differences kept Jan from concluding they were related, yet she couldn't dismiss the idea somehow there was a connection. The test results of the powder and the tablet found at the McConnell home would take more time than she would prefer. And calling for a rush job could result in analysis errors. Every detective's nightmare.

Jenny was meeting her friend Debbie again for another night of relaxation and drinks. Jan now wished she hadn't declined a second offer to join them. Maybe time away from the job *was* what she needed. Her friend, Crabby Phillips, had suggested a diversion in his roundabout way. On the other hand, she felt uneasy going to a bar with two young women, like a mother hen keeping a close watch on her chicks. And she still harbored the discomfort of not wanting to get that close to Jenny. Guilt of what had happened to Seeward still clung to her like a festering pustule. Her refusal to reveal the real reason for his taking matters into his own hands continued to affect her professional *and* personal life as well. She'd considered an appointment with employee assistance to seek the aid of a psychiatrist, but feared that word might be leaked. A private doctor was too expensive. Self-pity made her angry, and she cursed her weakness.

"Dammit! I *will* beat this guilty feeling *and* solve these murders." She released a heavy sigh, frustrated at her reluctance to see about getting some help.

CHAPTER 15

Three weeks passed with no break in the Corbett/McConnell cases. The autopsy on Amanda McConnell revealed strangulation had been the cause of her death, not the battering to her face. Jan's frustration escalated and, in time, bled into Jenny. Both of them became irritable and testy, and the working atmosphere with their fellow detectives became tense. Added to the misery was their inability to locate Jerry Scanlon. When they'd decided stopped by his apartment, they were informed by a neighbor Scanlon had not been around for days. Not one of the residents in the immediate vicinity considered him a friend or an acquaintance. No one knew where he had gone.

Other cases dropped into their laps. Sufficient evidence, credible witnesses, and good investigating brought them to a close. The reward satisfied the detectives for the time, but the Corbett/McConnell cases still haunted them.

One slow Friday afternoon found the pair engaged in filling out or reviewing reports. Jan eyed Jenny with slight agitation when her partner received what sounded like a personal phone call.

"Tyler, I asked you never to call me at work," Jenny said. She looked at Jan and mouthed, "my nephew." She then lowered her head as if she feared being scolded.

Eavesdropping always made Jan feel uneasy, so she set her eyes on her computer monitor.

"Okay, but we have to make it quick because I'm busy. And if I win, you know what I want. And you have to pay for it with your own money. Deal?"

Jan glanced at her and shifted in her chair.

"All right, what is it?" Jenny asked. "Do you have the answers in front of you?

Okay, here goes. Virginia, New Jersey, Massachusetts, New Hampshire, Pennsylvania, New York, Maryland, Connecticut, Rhode Island, Delaware, North Carolina, South Carolina, and Georgia." She paused then grinned. "I have to go now. I'm sorry I snapped at you, Tyler. I love you, too." She hung up and leaned back in her chair. Her grin widened into a self-satisfying smile.

Jan wore a scowl as she looked away from her computer monitor. "What was that all about?"

"I'm sorry, Jan, but my nephew and I play this game where we ask each other questions about math, history, science, or whatever. Whoever gets stumped has to reward the other. It helps him with his schoolwork."

"How old is he?"

"Ten."

"What on earth did he ask you?"

"To name the original thirteen colonies in the order in which they were founded."

"And you knew that?"

"History was one of my favorite subjects...even in college. I think my sister-in-law knows I've been on edge lately and told him to call me."

Jan was reminded of her favorite niece. A call from Riley Jo would definitely do her some good. Maybe she'd surprise her with a call when she got home. Curiosity prompted the next question. "So tell me, what did you win?"

Jenny beamed like an entitled teenager. "An orange smoothie."

Jan's smile faded to a reflective expression.

"What is it, Jan?"

"A crazy notion...and probably nothing. Jenny, call St. Pete Beach, Indian Rocks Beach, Indian Shores, any agency along the coast you can think of with its own police department. Ask them about any unsolved murders. And make sure you pay close attention to the dates the murders occurred."

The request confused the young detective, but she went straight to work.

CHAPTER 16

Scanlon lazed in the aluminum john boat and swatted away flies as he basked in the afternoon sun. His two weeks of rest and recuperation had gone well. His lip was almost healed, and only traces of the bruise under his right eye remained.

He'd taken to the slow and deliberate lifestyle of the small town. The friendliness of its residents helped him forget the pain and suffering he endured in the city. Here, it would be so easy to blend in and never be noticed. A lack of job opportunities was the only problem. Scarce since there weren't many pools. Country folks preferred to swim in the lakes and rivers. Prospects such as a driver for a delivery service or any kind of farm work wasn't a consideration due to his disability.

The end of his fishing pole arced several times, followed by the buzzing of the line as it left the reel. He bolted upright and grabbed the rod, playing the fish for a few seconds. Rock-hard resistance came next. "Is that all you got?" he taunted and laughed.

The thrill of competition, any kind of competition, brought him pleasure. He struggled like the novice he was and laughed again. The battle reminded him of the feisty blonde at the McConnell's house. Excitement surged through his body before he strangled her. This fish was a worthy adversary, but no match for a man with his upper body strength. Moments passed, and the battle continued until the fish grew tired, relented, and allowed him to hoist it aboard.

Scanlon dropped the good-sized bass to the bottom of the boat. He laid his boot across its gill flap, removed the hook from its mouth, and hoisted it to within inches of his face. "You have done well, brave warrior. Very well." He laughed again and kissed the fish, lowered it into the water, and allowed it to slip through his hands. A smart salute preceded him starting the motor and heading for shore. Monday, he decided, would be a good day to leave.

CHAPTER 17

Scanlon's only companion as he drove south on U.S. 41 was a star-filled sky. A lone pair of headlights slicing through the cool darkness was all he'd observed until he was five miles outside of Brooksville, where he met another motorist heading north.

He would be home and safely inside his apartment before his neighbors noticed he'd returned. He would avoid a boatload of questions about his time away and close the book on his absence. Rest was the best reason to exhaust the morning hours. Then he'd call his clients to reschedule appointments. What remained of the day would be used for the conception of another plan. The urge to fulfill his vengeful goal was growing stronger by the minute.

The turn onto State Road 54 brought more vehicles headed to wherever they needed to be. Scanlon knew he was well ahead of the madness of rush hour traffic. It would be an easy ride to St. Petersburg before he encountered the maze of roadways leading to Pass-a-Grille Beach.

His mind wandered back to the secluded cabin on Lake Bradley and he let go a wistful sigh. Although the rural getaway would be a wonderful place to hide after his mission was completed, he'd decided his final sanctuary must be miles away from the quiet haven of Floral City—many, many miles away.

He rolled into the driveway in front of his apartment as the rays of the morning sun spread across the sky. He removed his belongings and went inside, unseen and unheard, before his neighbors roused and prepared to go to work.

For the first time in quite a while, his leg felt fine. The time off from the rigors of his job had worked its magic. No longer forced to take an excessive number of pain pills helped clear his mind. But as good as he felt, he knew he would have to be wary of overconfidence and continue to be guarded and cautious in his actions.

CHAPTER 18

Jan entered the office shortly after six-thirty the next morning, hoping Jenny might already be there. A call to her partner the previous evening had crossed her mind, but the notion disappeared as the night wore on. She was delighted to see Jenny transfixed on the clue board as she sipped her coffee.

"Bucking for a promotion, Detective?" she said.

"What? Oh, good morning, Jan. I was just going over the information you had requested."

Jenny had added the names, locations, and dates of the murders she'd obtained from the other agencies on the beaches after eliminating those businesses without swimming pools or hot tubs. She had gone a step further by contacting some inland agencies.

"Did you find anything?"

Jenny continued to stare at the board. "Well, a little girl named Liza Glenn Yarborough was murdered in Indian Rocks Beach three weeks before we found Arthur Corbett. St. Pete Beach P.D. is working the case of an accountant named Elaine Fuller, which occurred ten days after Corbett, and, two days before, a couple named Gerard in Safety Harbor were found murdered."

"Safety Harbor?"

"The Gerards were found dead by their swimming pool like Amanda McConnell."

"Who's working that one?"

"Moore and Feinberg. I already exchanged information with them. And finally, Amanda McConnell in Seminole."

Jan sighed as a troublesome thought slipped into her mind. "Jenny, do we know if any of the victims are natives?"

"Florida natives?" The young detective went to her desk and grabbed her notepad. "Let's see…Yarborough was from Virginia. Her family was regular visitors, I was told. Fuller was from Massachusetts, and McConnell, from New York."

"The Gerards were the only victims born in Florida?"

"Oh! No, wait. Emma Gerard was born in Pennsylvania, and Anthony Gerard was born in New Hampshire."

As was her habit, Jan brought her left arm across her stomach, raised her right arm, and pulled on her chin.

"Jan, what are you seeing?"

"I'm not sure, and, to be honest, I'm grasping at straws. The game you played with your nephew. Start with Yarborough and go down the list in order until you get to the Gerards. Put his name before hers, then list the—"

"But I have them in order."

"Not by their names, Jenny, by their home states."

"Uh, okay. It would be Virginia, New Jersey, Massachusetts, New Hampshire…

Pennsylvania…New York…" Jenny's eyes widened. "Jan! It's the original thirteen colonies! The murders are being committed in the order in which the original thirteen colonies were founded."

"Maybe."

"What do you mean, *maybe*? It's all right there!"

Jan continued to study the board. "Okay, if it *is* true, then which state is next?"

"Maryland."

"All right. Now, will the victim from Maryland be a visitor or a resident? And do we have any idea where he or she might be living or staying?"

Jenny's blue eyes slowly lowered to the floor. "There's no way to tell."

"Remember, this is just a hunch, partner. I may be totally wrong. The locations of where the murders occurred offer no set pattern, but at least we *think* we know the next victim will be from Maryland."

Jenny slapped her notepad against her thigh. "I hate this! We have to wait for another murder to find out if we're right. What kind of sick puppy comes up with this crap?"

She turned and stormed away, slinging her notepad across her desk as she dropped down into her chair.

Jan understood her partner's frustration and anger. She wasn't happy with the hand they'd been dealt, either, but all they could do was continue with their investigation. And wait.

"Jenny, talk to Moore and Feinberg again and get as much information as you can on the Gerard case. If they question you about any ideas we might have, tell them we don't have any."

"But what about the thirteen colonies theory?"

"Jenny, look, *you* may not mind being the butt of a joke that isn't funny, but I do. Now please do as I ask. And while you're busy with that, I'm going to pay Mr. Scanlon another visit. We've waited on him long enough."

CHAPTER 19

Jan was relieved Jenny hadn't questioned her as to why she was breaking procedure by doing an interview alone. A bad habit she'd developed while working with her former partner, Seeward Sinclair. But she had noticed the look of uncertainty in Jenny's eyes.

She waited until after nine o'clock to go to Jerry Scanlon's apartment. Some interviewees deserved the courtesy of a phone call and every opportunity to cooperate, but she figured he'd forfeited the consideration by not contacting them. She knew it was a gamble to arrive unannounced. He might be on the job. Or still be away. Or he might be gone for good.

When she got to his apartment, she blocked the driveway when she saw the blue Ford pickup. As she walked by the truck and noticed the bed was empty, she stopped to place her hand on the hood. The cool metal told her it hadn't been driven in a while. She pulled out her badge, walked to the front door, and knocked twice. No response. She knocked again. Louder. Harder. She thought she heard someone inside. A moment later the door swung open.

"What is it?" The man was unkempt and half-asleep.

"Jerry Scanlon?"

"Yeah."

"I'm Detective Sergeant Larkin, Pinellas County Sheriff's Office." She held out her badge. "I'd like to ask you some questions."

Scanlon offered a blank stare. "Sure. Come on in."

Jan eyed him carefully as she followed him into the small apartment. His cut-off jeans were wrinkled as if he'd worn them to bed. His unbuttoned short-sleeved shirt looked too small for his well-developed torso. And he appeared to be favoring his left leg. The air conditioner was more than adequate for the size of the room and felt as cold as a meat locker.

She took a chair at his dinette table and opened her notepad. "You're a hard man to locate, Mr. Scanlon. When did you get home?"

"Last night. Late," he mumbled and sat down. "Around twelve-thirty or one o'clock, I guess."

"Why didn't you return my calls?"

"I forgot my phone."

"You were out of town a long time."

"Uh-huh."

"Being without your phone didn't bother you?"

"Not in the least."

"You have a pool maintenance business, correct? What's the name of it?"

"Crystal Clear Pool Service."

"Phone number?"

"You already have it."

"I just want to make certain I was dialing the right number."

He sighed and gave her his phone number.

Jan noted it, then looked up at him. His answers were short and direct. "You do pool work for the McConnells in Seminole, correct?"

"I have clients named McConnell who live in Seminole."

She noticed the thin scar on his lower lip and the faded bruise under his right eye she'd missed earlier due to the bad lighting. "Have you been in a fight?"

"What?"

"Your face."

"I fell getting out of a boat." He raised a hand to his lips.

"So you went fishing, huh?"

"I caught a couple of nice ones, too."

"Were they tasty?"

"I let them go. I just enjoy catching them."

"Mr. Scanlon, since you've been out of town you probably don't know the McConnell's granddaughter, Amanda, has been murdered."

Scanlon's mouth dropped opened and he sat up straight. "Oh, no. When did it happen?"

"About two weeks ago."

He looked away and shook his head. "I've got to call and give them my condolences."

"I understand you were supposed to clean their pool the same day. How come you didn't show?"

"What day?" he asked.

"The day Amanda was murdered."

Scanlon narrowed his eyes. "I had an argument with another client. I was so upset I came back here and packed. I'd been planning on getting away for some time, so I left town without keeping my appointment with the McConnells."

Jan noticed his voice didn't waver. He never blinked. Not even the flicker of an eyelid. "I'd like a list of your clients."

"I'll get back to you. I'm not thinking clearly right now. I just can't believe what happened to the McConnell's granddaughter."

Jan stared hard at him, searching, but saw no signs of deception. "Fine. I'll expect to hear from you in a day or so." She pulled a business card from her pants pocket as she rose. "Call me when that list is ready." She started for the door then stopped and turned back. "And don't take another vacation without checking with me first."

"I'm a suspect?"

Jan said nothing as she left the apartment.

CHAPTER 20

Jan sat down with Jenny after she got back to the office and recounted her meeting with Jerry Scanlon. "He had all the right answers, but he was cold. He'd been through it all before. Do we know if he has a record?"

"I'll run a search on him," Jenny said.

"He seemed genuinely moved when I mentioned Amanda McConnell. Most people get emotional when they hear that kind of news, but something about him... I don't know."

"Speaking of Amanda McConnell, the lab results proved the powder found near the body was Vicodin, like the tablet Dave Forbes found."

Jan pulled on her chin. "Call the McConnells and find out if either of them has a prescription for Vicodin."

"Already done. James McConnell takes it for the osteoarthritis in his hands. But the tablet we found is a larger dosage."

Jan went back to pulling her chin.

Jenny cleared her throat. "I've been thinking about Amanda McConnell."

"Oh?"

"Forbes pointed out the abrasions on her face, elbows, and knees, so it's a safe bet she put up a fight. The autopsy report concluded she died by strangulation. The report also noted bruising on her right hand."

Jan's mind clicked. "Jerry Scanlon had a cut on his lower lip.

And what was left of a bruise under his right eye."

"Now that's interesting."

"Wish we knew if Scanlon takes any medication."

Jenny picked up a fax from her desk. "Here's the report from Moore and Feinberg on the Gerard murders. Unfortunately, there were no clues or signs of forced entry. A neighbor reported seeing a man go back to the pool area, though."

"Was it Scanlon?"

"She didn't know. There was no name on the truck."

"Did she remember the color of the truck?"

"No, and before you ask, she didn't remember the time, either."

"Terrific. Well, Scanlon is supposed to send me a list of his clients."

"When?"

"When he recovers from the shock of hearing Amanda McConnell was murdered."

The detectives stared at one another.

"Sounds to me like you got punked, Jan."

"We'll see."

They had lunch delivered, continued to toss around ideas, and made calls to other agencies in search of more information. By five-thirty, both were exhausted and decided nothing more could be done.

After much thought, Jan decided to forgo a previous decision she'd made about not getting close to another partner. "Jenny, I was thinking of grabbing a beer. Care to join me?"

"Really?"

"You've asked me twice, and... Well, I know this nice little place in Treasure Island."

Her partner's eyes brightened. "Jan, I'd love to."

CHAPTER 21

Once they'd left their cars in the parking lot of the Spinnaker Bar and Grill and started toward the front door, Jan felt obligated to offer her partner a mild heads-up. "This is my favorite watering hole. It may not be your kind of place, Jenny, but I feel at ease here."

"If you like it, then I'm sure I will," Jenny said.

They passed through the oak door and paused a few seconds for their eyes to adjust.

A crowd larger than Jan had expected filled the room. She spied a vacant booth in the rear. "Go grab that last booth, Jenny. I'll be with you in a minute."

Jenny seemed captivated by the laid-back atmosphere. And the crowd.

"What is it?" Jan said.

"Some of these people are old enough to be my parents."

"Just give it a chance. I think you'll enjoy it."

Jenny exhaled. "Okay."

"I'll only be a minute. I need to talk to Crabby and Hank."

Amid the rambunctious chatter and laughter drifting through the smoky air, Jan watched her skirt the booths and sit down in the last one. After greeting Crabby and Hank, she and the old seafarer strolled up to the booth.

"Jenny, I'd like you to meet Crabby Phillips. Crabby, this is Jenny Lester."

"Hi, Crabby."

Crabby doffed his captain's hat. "How do."

"Take care of him while I get us some beers," Jan said. "What are you drinking?"

"A Sedona Light, please," Jenny said.

Crabby and Jan looked at one another in mock surprise. "Sedona Li-i-i-ight," they sang.

Jenny laughed.

Crabby slid his hat back on his head. "I'll takes a‒‒"

"I *know* what you want," Jan said and nodded to Jenny. "I'll be right back." She smiled at the people sitting at the tables nearest their booth on her way to the bar.

Hank was wiping down the counter. "Who's that sitting with Crabby, Jan?" he said.

"Her name's Jenny Lester, my new partner."

"How is she working out?"

"She's doing a fine job."

"Looks like they're hitting it off."

"I thought she might like to meet him... and you, too."

Hank grinned. "What'll you have?"

"Two shots, two beers, and a Sedona Light."

"A Sedona Light?" Hank arched his eyebrows.

Jan shrugged.

"Okay, I'll bring them right over."

"Let me do it, Hank. You've got your hands full at the bar."

While Hank was rounding up their drinks, Jan turned to watch her partner and the old salt converse. Both of them appeared relaxed and enjoying themselves. Then Jenny lost her smile. *Uh oh*, she thought. *I wonder what that's all about?*

"Here you go, Jan," Hank said.

Focused on Jenny and Crabby, Jan didn't answer.

"Jan?"

"Oh! Thanks, Hank."

"Is there something wrong?"

"I don't think so." Jan glanced over her shoulder at them.

"Crabby's probably telling her one of his fish tales." She picked up the drinks, clutching the tray with both hands. As she started back to the booth, she contemplated what Crabby had really been telling Jenny. Maybe about the first time they met? She caught part of what Crabby was saying as she neared them.

"She's a good person, Jenny," he said. "She jus' needs ta...well...I guess ya heard 'bout t'other fella she worked with."

Jenny started to answer, but stopped when she saw Jan.

Jan set their drinks on the table, slid the Sedona Light to Jenny, a shot and a mug to Crabby, and then sat down in front of the second shot and beer. She lifted her glass for a toast. "May your trawl nets always be full."

She and Crabby brought their glasses together.

Jenny watched as they downed the shots in perfect synchronization and chased them with generous amounts of beer.

"Oh, that do taste good," Crabby said.

Jenny looked at her bottle, then took a healthy pull.

Crabby smiled when Jan winked at him.

"Jenny, did you want a shot?"

"No, thanks, Jan. I'm not that bold."

"So how goes it?" Crabby asked.

"Not so well," Jan said. "We're stuck with two murders and very little to go on." She stared at her empty shot glass. "I don't really want to talk about it."

Crabby picked up his mug and drank some of his beer.

Jan ran a finger around the top of her glass. "Crabby, tell Jenny about the shark."

Jenny's blue eyes went wide. "What shark?"

"Oh, I dunno, Jan. Some people gets a might skitterish when they hears muh story."

"Go on, Crabby. She can handle it."

Jenny leaned forward as the old salt began to weave his tale.

"I's 'bout your age, I guess. Worked on a fishin' boat outta Mad Beach. That's what we called Madeira Beach back then. We was lookin' fer grouper 'bout, oh, two hunnert miles out.

The *Middle Grounds* they calls it. It's 'bout halfway b'tween the Atwater Valley an' the Lloyd Ridge. Anyway, we found ourselves smack dab in the middle o' the largest school o' grouper I'd ever seed. Well, then we started bringin' 'em in. Thousands of 'em. An' we was all feelin' real good 'bout ourselves. I gotta little cocky an' started ta dance around the deck. Somehow, I lost muh footin' and fell overboard."

Jenny leaned a little closer.

"The boat was 'bout twenty-five, thirty yards away from me afore anybody knowed what happent. The guys was all yellin', so I starts swimmin' as best I could. All of a sudden, I hears somebody yell, 'Shark!' I looks behind me an' sees this fin a-cuttin'

through the water."

"What kind of shark was it, Crabby?" Jenny asked.

"Bull shark. Big fella, too. Eight or nine foot, an' as mean as they come. So there 'e is a-comin' right fer me, so I stops swimmin'. They's attracted ta noise, ya know. Anyway, 'e turns ta the right an' starts a-circlin' me, real slow-like. Musta been feedin'

on them grouper an' thought I's the biggest o' the bunch. Then afore I knows it, he turns an' starts a-headin' straight fer me."

"Oh, no."

"Now, I'd always heared if ya hits a shark, they'll turn and run. So I kicks him in the snout an' swims away as fast as I could. Then I hears somebody yell, 'He's right b'hind ya!' So I stops swimmin' an' looks back. Well, there 'e is, bigger'n life, an' a-comin' at me again. So I kicks him again. By now, I'm pert near the boat, so the guys throws me a rope. When they was a-haulin' me in, I lost muh grip an' fell back inta the water."

"What happened next?"

"After I went under, I opens muh eyes an' sees bull shark a-comin' at me real fast. Now most people don't know this, Jenny, but right afore a shark hits, they turns sideways so's they kin wrap them jaws around ya."

Jenny gasped. "What did you do?"

Crabby took a pull of beer. "I got et."

"You got...what?"

Jan burst into laughter as the old fisherman smiled and revealed his yellow-

stained teeth.

Jenny looked at Jan, then back at Crabby. "Ha. Ha. Very funny. You two are a couple of regular comedians." She shook her head and laughed with them.

The beer and laughter continued well into the evening.

Jan gave no further thought that night to the pair of unsolved murders and the disappointment she'd felt earlier.

CHAPTER 22

June arrived with an inferno of heat and humidity. Even the natives couldn't recall the last time such a blistering had taken place. The days were sweltering and tempers were short. Through all of it, Scanlon felt a different kind of heat. Three days past the surprise visit from the detective, he had yet to supply her with his list of clients. He knew he couldn't ignore her forever. And a partial list was not an option. She might discover some of the names were missing and conclude he was hiding something. He would have to give her the complete list and hope for the best.

Since his vengeful mission began, he'd harbored an uneasy feeling. Anxiety that fate might play a hand in his discovery created suspicion deep down inside him. Except for the pain pill he'd stepped on at the McConnell's house, he'd been careful not to be seen or leave any incriminating evidence behind. He knew old man McConnell took Vicodin. He'd even borrowed a few tabs on occasion, so he felt relatively certain he was safe. There was no set pattern to the murders, the methods were of question, and multiple agencies were involved. Even though some of the deceased were his clients, there was no connection between him and the other victims. Still, he could tell the female detective was smart enough to employ every investigative method available. Never underestimate your opponent, his high school football coach had preached. A lesson he never forgot.

He was a block away from his appointment in Oldsmar when his phone rang.

"Jerry Scanlon, please."

"Yeah, it's me."

"This is Detective Sergeant Larkin, Pinellas County Sheriff's Office."

"Yeah."

"Do you always answer your business phone that way?"

"Is that why you called?"

"Mr. Scanlon, I haven't received your list of clients yet. Is there a problem?"

"No problem here. I dropped it in the mail this morning."

"I see. Why didn't you text the list to me? Or send an e-mail. My address is on the business card I gave you."

"I don't text, and I don't have a computer."

"Really? I thought everyone had joined the Information Age."

"You've been to my apartment. I don't exactly live in the lap of luxury."

"Mr. Scanlon, is something bothering you? I get the feeling I caught you at a bad time."

"I'm sorry, Detective. It's this heat. I'm trying to catch up on my work. I'm sure you'll have the list in a day or so."

"Thank you. I'll keep an eye out for it."

Now I'll have to send the list, he thought.

The question rolling around in his mind was whether to move forward with number seven. Maybe he should wait another week. Or a month. He shook his head in an effort to thwart the growth of uncertainty.

CHAPTER 23

Jan put down the receiver. Was Scanlon jacking her around on purpose? It was obvious he didn't like cops. On the other hand, maybe he was short-changed in the intelligence department, as Jenny suggested. Maybe not.

"I really don't like this Jerry Scanlon at all," she mumbled.

"What did you say?" Jenny asked.

"Oh, just thinking out loud."

"About Scanlon?"

"What do we know about him?"

Jenny's fingers danced over her computer keyboard. "Here it is. Jefferson Gerald Scanlon, twenty-six. Single, high school graduate, two and a half years of college, where he majored in history. Self-employed, and he rents a place in St. Pete Beach. The usual lists of debts. There is a record of him being in an automobile accident. No arrests, though. That's about it. To look at this, he's pretty clean."

"An automobile accident? When did it happen?"

Jenny focused on the keyboard and then on the monitor. "Jan, come look at this."

Jan circled around to her partner's desk.

A photograph of two mangled cars tangled in the middle of an intersection filled the screen.

"What a mess," Jan said. "And Scanlon lived through that?"

Jenny scrolled down. "This article from the *Hillsborough*

Courier says Scanlon was badly injured, mostly to his left leg. The other driver, later determined to be intoxicated, was killed."

"Does it say who was at fault?

Jenny pulled up the accident report again. "Two witnesses said the other driver ran a red light."

"Anything else?"

"He played for the USF football team. The accident ended his season."

"I wonder if it ended his season permanently."

"Let's see…Yep, here it is. He was a star player, Jan. A later article says the accident ended his chances of playing professional football."

"And now he cleans pools. No wonder he has a rotten attitude."

"Hmm."

"Yes?"

"The article says his name is Jeff Scanlon."

"Is it another Scanlon?"

Jenny searched. "No, his full name is Jefferson Gerald Scanlon."

"Interesting. Wonder why he goes by Jerry now?"

Jenny shrugged.

Jan started to turn away, then stopped. "You know, Jenny, an injury that serious most likely limits a person's ability to get around."

"He doesn't seem to have a problem cleaning pools."

"Remember I told you when I first went into his apartment, it looked like he was favoring his left leg."

"The left side of his body took the brunt of the impact in the crash."

"Now I'm really wondering if he takes medication for pain."

"It'll be next to impossible to get a hold of his medical records."

"Yeah, I suppose so." Jan continued to peruse the accident report.

Jenny's blue eyes widened. "Are you thinking he killed Amanda McConnell?"

"The powder and pill found on the McConnell's pool deck was pain medication, right?"

"Both were Vicodin, but remember, Mr. McConnell has a prescription for Vicodin. He has osteoarthritis in his hands."

"Did Mrs. McConnell tell you the dosage?"

"Five milligrams, and she said he's good about not taking too many."

"How about the pill you found?"

"It was ten milligrams. Maybe the higher dosage tabs belonged to the granddaughter."

"Could be. I wonder if her grandparents would know." Jan paused. "I sure wish we could find out if Scanlon was popping pills, though."

Jenny said nothing, but Jan could tell by the distant look in her eyes her mind was elsewhere. She waved her hand in front of her partner's face.

"Hello? Is anybody in there?"

"What? Oh! Yeah! I was just thinking. I have an acquaintance who is an internet technician. This person is very good at getting information that is hard to come by, if you know what I mean."

"I know exactly what you mean, Detective, and I can't believe you would even suggest such a thing."

Jenny lowered her head. "Sorry, Jan."

"Let's at least wait until we're desperate."

A grin shaped Jenny's mouth when she looked up.

Unlike her partner, Jan's lighthearted expression faded to pensive.

"Working on another plan?" Jenny said.

"I'll let you know when we get a look at Scanlon's client list." Jan huffed. "I'm beat. Let's call it a day."

Jenny cleared the information from her computer monitor.

"Any big plans tonight?" Jan said.

"I think I'll stay home and read, then turn in early."

"No barhopping with Debbie?"

"Her cousin, Sue, is in town."

"And they didn't invite you to go along?"

Jenny looked down at her desk. "They did, but when they get together, they talk about family and things they did when they were kids. I always feel like an outsider."

"Well, how about you and I relax with a few beers, then get some dinner?"

Jenny slowly raised her head. "Thanks, Jan, but I think I'll just head home." She glanced around the room. "Could I talk to you?"

"Sure."

"You were married, right? And probably had your share of boyfriends?"

"I was married. But as far as my share of boyfriends, it wasn't a large share."

"I don't seem to be able to attract any decent guys. I mean, when they find out I'm a cop, they disappear. I've dated a few cops, but it never seems to work out."

"Work out in what way?"

"I'd like to get married, Jan. You know, like normal people. I guess I'm just feeling sorry for myself. It's just sometimes I get so lonely."

"Jenny, we all go through that at one time or another. You're an intelligent, attractive woman. And you're good at what you do. So, you're a cop. So what? If some guys can't handle it, that's their problem. My ex couldn't handle it. A lot of people, men *and* women, can't handle having a relationship with a cop. It's a burden we have to bear. But believe me, he's out there somewhere. You'll find him."

"Thanks, Jan. You're a good friend."

Jan smiled, but a sense of betrayal began a slow rise inside her. She was getting too close to her partner.

CHAPTER 24

Later that week during the heat of the day, Scanlon was testing the pH balance of the water in the gated swimming pool at the Sunny Days Retirement Center. Drenched with sweat, he looked up and spied Nelda Williams as she neared him. He smiled when he noticed the bottle of water she in her hand and stopped working.

"Mrs. Williams, how are you today?"

"Fine, Jerry. I brought you some water. It's so dreadfully hot today."

"Thank you. I can sure use it."

"I just finished baking some of your favorite chocolate chip cookies."

Scanlon smiled and pulled a blue bandana from the left rear pocket of his shorts. "You spoil me, Mrs. Williams."

"They're cooling in my apartment. Would you like to come up and have a few after you're done with the pool? That is, if you have the time."

"I always have time for your cookies. I'll be right up as soon as I'm finished."

"Oh, good!" She left him with a smile.

He watched her scurry away, then wiped his face and stuffed the bandana to his pocket as he returned to work. His next course of action would take some thought.

Security cameras were mounted at each entrance. In no way

would his presence in the building go unnoticed. He looked at his watch and noted the time was 4:40 p.m. The front desk monitors changed shifts at five o'clock, and Nina would be on duty soon. Perfect. Good old absent-minded Nina. She wouldn't give him a second look. At best, she would forget she'd even seen him.

He loaded the tool bag into his truck then walked to the exit door in the rear of the building. A buzzer announced his request to enter. He looked up and smiled at the camera, offering a friendly wave of his hand. Familiar with the sound of the lock as it released, he swung the aluminum door open.

Relieved to find the elevator empty of passengers, he hoped it wouldn't stop before reaching the sixth floor. Luck was on his side as he stepped into the hallway and looked in both directions. His sneakers and the well-worn aquamarine carpet allowed him to make his way in silence.

Standing alone in front of Apartment 605, he steadied himself and knocked. Little time passed before the door was opened.

"Hello, Jerry. Please come in."

"Thank you, Mrs. Williams."

The elderly woman's home was a modestly furnished one-bedroom dwelling, painted in cheerful pastel yellows and blues. The walls were filled with pictures of her family.

"Have a seat at the table, and I'll get your cookies," she said. "Would you like some milk? Cold milk goes good with my chocolate chip cookies."

Scanlon offered his friendliest smile. "You read my mind, Mrs. Williams."

The kindly woman went to the kitchen, returning at once with a plate of cookies, a glass of milk, and a brown paper bag. "Here you are." She set the bag on the table in front of him. "Take these home with you."

"They smell wonderful. I'll bet they taste just as good." He picked up a cookie from the plate and began to eat it, quickly cutting a glance around the room. "I see your family is with you."

"Yes, I am very fortunate to have such fine children and grandchildren. They all live in Hampstead, Maryland, where I'm from originally. Would you like to see my photo album?"

"Sure."

He popped the last piece of cookie into his mouth.

When she returned, she was focused on the album. "Here's my favorite picture of the entire...Jerry? Are you all right?"

He got to his feet but said nothing and glared at her. A burning anger consumed him. A hatred of anyone not born in Florida.

"Jerry, you don't look well."

"You're just like all the rest."

The impact from his fist exploded across the left side of her face, knocking her off her feet. In the next instant, he stepped to the sofa and grabbed a throw pillow before she could move. Dropping down on top of her, he pressed the pillow over her face.

"Fight me, you bitch!" he growled and pushed the pillow down harder.

The woman didn't move.

When his loathing of all tourists subsided, he lifted the pillow and discovered he'd broken her nose. Blood was streaming down the right side of her face. He tossed the pillow back onto the sofa as he stood up and struggled to control his breathing. Several seconds later, his mind clicked.

He hurried to the table, grabbed the plate, and dumped the cookies into the bag. Scooping up the glass of milk, he went to the sink. Once he'd poured the milk down the drain, he rinsed the plate and the glass and dried them. He placed the pair in the cabinet above the sink with the others, careful to wipe clean the cabinet handle with the dish towel. A quick scan of the kitchen preceded him moving to the front door. He glanced at the body of the old woman, then wrapped the bottom of his T-shirt around his hand. Every inch of the doorknob needed to be wiped clean before he left.

The hallway was empty. He quick-stepped to the elevator and was about to hit the button when he stopped. The stairs would be slower for him, but the chance his escape would be interrupted was less likely. Again, he used his T-shirt to cover his hand and pulled open the fire escape door.

Each step down the stairs was difficult given his gimpy leg, but as he reached the first floor, he checked his watch. 5:09 p.m. He paused to catch his breath, readied himself, then eased the door open. The immediate vicinity was vacant. He made his exit on quiet feet. A short and casual stroll to his truck fed the sensation of giddiness that always accompanied a successful mission. The tantalizing rush of beating the odds once more.

CHAPTER 25

Jan removed a folded sheet of paper from the envelope addressed to her and studied it. "Jenny, I've got the client list from Scanlon." She flipped it across her desk to her partner. "Check it against the names of the victims. All of them."

Jenny got up and walked to the clue board. Several minutes passed.

"Jan, we have some matches."

"Let's hear them."

"The condo in Madeira Beach where we found Arthur Corbett, The McConnell home in Seminole, and the Gerard home in Safety Harbor."

"What about the rest?"

"I've already checked the Island Song Cottages in Indian Rocks Beach where Liza Yarborough was murdered. They don't have a pool. The Four Winds in St. Pete Beach where Elaine Fuller was staying isn't on the list either."

Disappointment soured the air between the detectives.

Jan folded her arms and leaned back.

Jenny watched her a moment, then went back to checking the list.

Time went into slow motion as the pair huddled together to process every idea, every possibility, and every hunch they could imagine. Some sounded good, some even promising, but none convinced them to put the finger on Scanlon.

Frustration led Jan to return to her desk.

Jenny finally abandoned the clue board for her desk and stared at her computer monitor without hesitation.

Jan wondered what had taken control of her partner's thoughts this time. She continued to watch her in silence.

The young detective began a determined pounding on the keyboard. Moments passed before she stopped and wheeled her chair from the side of the monitor.

"Jan, the Six Mile Reef motel in Indian Rocks Beach is two doors down from the Island Song Cottages. The Lost Treasure motel in St. Pete Beach is next door to the Four Winds Resort hotel."

"And they're both on Scanlon's list."

"You win the lottery. If he didn't work at each crime scene, he certainly was in the vicinity."

"Good job, Jenny, but I'm afraid a first-year attorney wouldn't think much of your discovery. In each case, his presence is circumstantial."

"But his reason for being there gave him the opportunity to select a victim."

"Jenny, we have no clues, no murder weapons, and no witnesses."

Jenny narrowed her eyes. "It's him, Jan. I know it's him. I can feel it."

"I'm with you, but the sad fact is we have nothing that ties him to any of the murders."

"I'm going to find out the dates and times he was at each place, anyway."

"Fine, but do it tomorrow morning. If the information looks promising, we'll pay Jerry Scanlon another visit. And this time we'll squeeze him a little more."

Jenny rubbed her hands together. "I can't wait."

CHAPTER 26

With only two appointments scheduled for the day, Scanlon was looking forward to a later start to his workday. His customers had expressed no need for urgency, so he figured he'd leave sometime around mid-morning. A restless night had chased away the rest he'd needed. The old woman's face continued to haunt him. He finally gave up in the last hour before dawn and climbed out of bed.

Unlike the initial surge of excitement he always felt, no trace of satisfaction or accomplishment had lingered. He'd never experienced the emptiness that followed. The old woman made no attempt to fight back. Why? Even the old man on the beach had taken a swing at him. And a feeling he'd overlooked a matter of importance persisted in nagging him. Not the security cameras. Residents and staff always recognized him. But something he'd neglected in his urgency to leave the building.

With his morning routine of three Vicodin and two cups of coffee completed, he took his time getting dressed. He decided a large breakfast, followed by a slow ride to the Oldsmar home of his first client, would be a nice way to begin the day. As he secured the tool bag in the back of his truck, he felt his stomach grumble. French toast and sausage with a side order of biscuits and gravy would satisfy his hunger.

It's been a while since I've had shingles with pigs in slop, he thought.

Smiling to himself, he fired up his Ford pickup and headed toward the Schuler Family Restaurant a few blocks away.

As he backed into the street, the icy grip of realization latched onto his spine and twisted his stomach into a knot. He'd forgotten to grab the bag of cookies on the old woman's dining table. Disgusted, he cursed himself for being so stupid. A sinking feeling followed, and his inner voice delivered a frank and unsettling message.

They know it's you.

CHAPTER 27

En route to Jerry Scanlon's apartment, Jan noticed an unusual lack of enthusiasm in Jenny. After her fifth cup of coffee before they left the office, she'd asked Jan to drive. The coffee hadn't kept her partner from dozing off several times between yawns. The temptation was too much for the veteran detective to resist.

"Did we have a late night, Detective?" she said.

Jenny yawned again. "I was bad."

Jan laughed and nudged her partner. "Friend Debbie and her cousin kidnap you and force you to party?"

"I went voluntarily. But they *are* guilty of employing deception."

"How so?"

"They took me dancing."

This admission brought more laughter from Jan. "And how was that deceiving you?"

"Debbie knows I love to dance. When I get started, I don't know when to stop."

Once they'd arrived at the pool cleaner's apartment, it was obvious Scanlon wasn't home.

"Damn! His truck's not here," Jan said. "Well, let's check out his place anyway, just to be sure."

They walked to the front of the apartment and tried to look through the windows.

The panes were hazed over with salt and grime.

Jan attempted to call Scanlon, but received his voice mail for her effort.

"I'm really not liking this guy," she groused.

Frustrated their endeavor to surprise Scanlon had been a bust, the detectives began the long ride back to the office, unaware a message from the Treasure Island Police Department awaited them.

CHAPTER 28

Jan had looked forward to Sundays, always a good day to relax. This Sunday, though, she was about to break two of her personal hard and fast rules. She'd already broken one rule by leaving Jenny in the office to interview a suspect alone. Her attempt to confront Jerry Scanlon alone for a second time would have her sidestepping procedure again, along with violating another principle. She hadn't informed Jenny of what she was about to do. She figured her effort was unlikely to be successful, anyway. The fate of her former partner flashed through her mind.

The morning had begun with lines of coal-black clouds rolling in from the Gulf of Mexico. Sheets of quarter-sized drops pelted everything in their path. The deluge was unmerciful as streets became rivers. Sand, debris, and whatever else in the storm's path that was unsecured was swept away by currents down the nearest storm drain. The cells soon departed, only to be followed by the next wave of rain, typical of Florida weather in the summer.

Jan eyed Scanlon's truck in the driveway as she waited in her car for another downpour and checked her Glock 17. When the next heavy shower began, she shoved the automatic into the holster clipped to her slacks and steeled herself. A moment later, she left her car.

Similar to what had happened on her first visit, a brief delay after she knocked preceded him opening the door.

Scanlon stood zombie-like and wiped the sleep from his eyes. "You again?"

"I have some more questions."

"What, today? Right now?" He groaned and glanced at the sky.

"I left you a message yesterday morning. You didn't call me back."

Scanlon drew his face into a scowl and threw the door open wider. He turned his back on her and hobbled to the small dining table near the wall.

For a second time, she noticed his limp.

"What happened to your leg?"

"Football injury," he said and sat down.

Jan knew that was a lie and wondered how many other lies he'd told her. She took a seat in the chair across from him.

"I was looking over your list of clients and noticed some of them are dead."

Scanlon's eyes held no signs of emotion.

"That's somewhat unusual, don't you think?"

"Detective, I have no idea of what you're talking about?"

"The Gerards in Safety Harbor and the McConnell's granddaughter."

Scanlon cocked his head to the right. "The Gerards are dead?"

"You didn't know?"

"How would I?"

"You cleaned their pool the day they were murdered."

"They were fine when I left."

"What about Amanda McConnell?"

"What about her?"

Jan narrowed her eyes. "You were supposed to clean the McConnell's pool the same day, weren't you?"

Scanlon returned her glare. "I believe we already went over that."

"That was before we received some new information. Some powder was discovered on the pool deck. Analysis has proven it was a painkiller. Do you take any medication for your leg?"

"So what if I do?"

"Is that a yes?"

"Yes, Detective. I take medication for my leg."

"What do you take?"

"Vicodin, but I'm sure you already know that. And I'm guessing you know Mr. McConnell takes it for his arthritis." Scanlon held up his right hand and wiggled his fingers.

"We found a tablet near Amanda's body that didn't belong to him."

Scanlon sighed. "Every so often I give him some of my tabs. Yes, they *are* stronger than his dosage, but sometimes he runs out and needs relief."

"That's very generous of you. I'm sure your medication isn't cheap. Plus, it's against the law since it's a narcotic".

. "So, I'm guilty of trying to help the man."

"Uh-huh. And you say you were at the Gerard's home, but they were alive when you left?"

"That's right."

"Did you see anyone hanging around the neighborhood? You know, like someone you hadn't seen before?"

"No."

Jan knew she wasn't going to get any more out of him, so she decided to end the interview. She thanked him for his time and was almost out the door when she thought to ask him one last question.

"Oh, Mr. Scanlon, one of your clients is the Sunny Days Retirement Center, correct?"

"Yeah."

"We got a call from the Treasure Island Police Department. It seems a Nelda Williams was found dead yesterday afternoon in her apartment."

"It's a retirement home, Detective. I suspect they find residents dead from time to time."

"You cleaned their pool yesterday afternoon, right?"

Scanlon nodded.

"You were also seen entering and leaving the building."

Scanlon shook his head and laughed.

"Something funny, Mr. Scanlon?"

"Detective, you may find this hard to believe, but I do have to use the restroom on occasion. Anything else?"

"No, that's all."

"Then can I ask you a couple of questions?"

"Certainly."

"Do you think some of my clients might employ yard maintenance companies?"

His query caught her off guard, but Jan didn't flinch. "I would say so."

"Then tell me, are you as interested in those contractors as you are in me?"

Jan turned her back on him and walked out into the rain.

CHAPTER 29

Jan didn't tell Jenny she'd initiated a surprise visit to interview Jerry Scanlon until early Monday afternoon. She soon discovered being excluded did not sit well with her partner.

"With all due respect, Sergeant, weren't you the one who insisted we keep the lines of communication open at all times?"

Jan offered a brief nod. "I did, and I promise it won't happen again."

"What did you find out?"

Jan told her the answers to the pointed questions she'd asked Scanlon had been terse and unemotional.

"I've often wondered what could drive a person to kill someone without feeling any remorse or guilt," Jenny said.

"I don't know. And I hope I never feel that way."

They went over the information supplied by the Treasure Island Police Department concerning the Nelda Williams murder again.

The likeable grandmother had been seen by a neighbor going into her apartment sometime late in the afternoon. She had been spotted by a janitor a short time later, heading out of the rear exit carrying a bottle of water. A friend, Laura Smeaton, confirmed Mrs. Williams often baked cookies for the staff and maintenance people.

They had found a bag of cookies on the dining table, but no one knew how long they'd been there or who they were for.

Nothing had been stolen from the apartment. The only items that appeared out of place were a family photo album lying on the floor and the bloody pillow determined to have been used to smother the elderly lady. The left side of her face had been badly bruised and her nose broken, the result a dark red splash of dried blood filling her right ear.

"The forensics report says no foreign DNA was present," Jenny said,

"Figures."

"Interesting, though, is that the police report says her friend, Laura Smeaton, confirmed Williams almost always gave cookies, chocolate chip cookies, to her favorite visiting worker."

"Don't tell me," Jan said. "Her favorite cookie monster was Jerry Scanlon."

"Smeaton said she never missed an opportunity to talk to him. And the cookies in the bag found on her table were chocolate chip."

"Please tell me the security cameras put him inside the building during the time of the attack."

"Smiling directly at the camera before he entered the rear exit door. And he left the same way a little after five o'clock."

"But he didn't have the cookies."

"The fact he was even in the building makes him look suspicious, but that doesn't prove he killed her." Jenny paused. "Jan, according to the report, the security camera showed Scanlon waiting to use the elevator after he entered. But later he came through the door to the stairwell when he left. Why would he use the stairs?"

"I don't know. Maybe he needed the exercise."

Jenny's response was a contorted and ugly expression.

"Not buying it, huh? Okay, if I'm Scanlon, I'd tell you I got tired of waiting for the elevator."

"And you took the stairs with a bad leg?"

"Good point, partner. Something else just occurred to me.

Scanlon implied he went inside the building to use the restroom. What reason would he have to use the elevator or the stairs? There must be a public restroom on the first floor."

"He's got to be lying. Let's hope Treasure Island P.D. can prove he was in Nelda Williams' apartment."

Proof of Scanlon's whereabouts was certainly a cause for concern, but the message her partner's body language sent set Jan to wondering. Subtle habits all people possessed were what made them unique.

"Anything else we need to discuss?" she said.

"I don't think so."

"Having doubts about what you're having for lunch?"

Jenny grinned. "I was just thinking about Debbie."

"Your friend? Is she in some kind of trouble?"

"She and her cousin went out again Saturday night. They asked me to go, but I didn't feel like it. Yesterday morning, Debbie called to say she'd met a guy at the club. He was handsome, clever, and quite the gentleman. They danced a little, but talked mostly, and she could tell he was interested."

"Sounds like she had an enjoyable evening. Are they going to see each other again?"

"That's just it, Jan. Debbie gave him her phone number. I told her she shouldn't have done that. She just met him."

"Is Debbie eager for a relationship?"

"Too eager. I've talked to her about it before. There are too many whack jobs in the world today. You have to be extra careful."

"I agree, but most people don't have a jaded view of society like you and me. They like to see the good side of people."

"And that's Debbie. Super positive about everything."

"It may be a good idea to talk to her again."

"I will, Jan. I want to find out more about this guy."

Jan hoped Jenny's friend would realize the serious consequences that might arise from making a bad decision.

CHAPTER 30

For many years, the tropical paradise of Florida had been a haven for escapees from the northern and midwestern parts of the country. Starting in November, visitors poured in for weeks and sometimes months at a time until after Easter, when they began their migration home. June began the season of the hurricanes, a time for natives and transplants alike to be mindful of the weather. The temperature of the Gulf waters rose along with the humidity and made conditions ideal for nature to unleash one of its furies. Quick-developing systems in the Caribbean or Gulf gave little notice to those unfortunate enough to lie in their path. In August and September, the systems rolled off the coast of Africa and headed wherever the fronts and jet streams led them.

Tropical Storm Gloria began as a depression below Cuba and moved into the Gulf of Mexico four days later as a Category One hurricane. She headed northwest at an easy pace of eight miles an hour with eighty-five degree waters would fuel forecasters predicting her intensity and help her reach Category Two a day or so later. A front moving east across Texas would persuade her to move to the northeast. By the time she made the predicted landfall somewhere between the Big Bend area and Weeki Wachee Springs, she could be a Category Three hurricane. Only two hundred miles off Florida's west coast, she was already releasing bands of showers that pounded Naples and Ft. Myers.

Scanlon watched Gloria with great interest. Although the weather in the Tampa Bay area had not yet been affected, he figured another notch in his belt could be achieved before the hurricane hit—wherever it hit—and act as the perfect cover amidst a time of confusion. He knew his next candidate, Drew Mitchell, the friendly young manager who worked the night shift for the Indian Shores motel, would be on the desk. If Gloria hit below Weeki Wachee Springs, a mandatory evacuation of the beaches would be imposed. Regardless, some folks refused to leave, and there were always deaths attributed to the hurricanes. It would take authorities quite some time to figure out exactly what had happened.

Mitchell would be the easiest of all his victims to lure into a trap. Often Scanlon caught him as he stared. He would hang around and engage in small talk after his shift ended, overly affable while Scanlon was cleaning the pool. He offered bottled water and laughed at every moronic joke. Not long after, he complimented Scanlon's chiseled physique in an off-hand way, confirming his attraction was genuine. Simple manipulation had gotten Mitchell to admit he was from Norwich, Connecticut. He became the obvious choice.

Scanlon laughed out loud as he drank his iced tea and watched the fronds of the palm trees in front of his apartment waving wildly. A steady twenty-mile-per-hour-wind blew warm across his face and served to assist the white cottonball clouds racing across the blue Florida sky. He felt good again, even though his leg ached from another day's work. He took a healthier drink and thought about the girl he'd met at the nightclub. She'd been eager to talk to him. So much he'd felt a degree of disgust. But she was attractive and maybe he could get laid before he left town. He set down his glass and picked up his phone.

"Jeff! I'm surprised you called," Debbie said. "I mean, I was hoping you'd call."

"Is this a bad time to talk?"

"Well, I am at work, but I can talk for a few minutes."

"Then I'll make this quick. I was thinking if we catch a break with this weather, then we might go out. Uh, I mean, would you like to? Go out, I mean? Like to dinner or a movie, maybe?"

She laughed. "I'd love to."

"Great! I was hoping you'd say that. How about I call you later? Today, I mean. Uh, say around six or six-thirty, maybe?"

"Wonderful. I'll be waiting."

Scanlon laid down his phone and picked up his iced tea, silently laughing to himself. His nervous suitor act had been a successful deception. Getting her into bed would be easier than he'd imagined.

Hurricane Gloria drifted further west before making a gradual turn to the northeast. As predicted, she became a Category Three storm with sustained winds of one hundred twenty-five miles per hour. There was a good possibility she would make landfall early Thursday morning. That would give Scanlon the window of opportunity he needed.

His offer to Debbie had been met with enthusiasm, but when he'd called her later, he'd suggested they postpone their date for a day or two. He heard the disappointment in her voice as she agreed. Recommending the delay had raised a level of frustration in him.

Besides her pleasant demeanor, he was drawn to her natural beauty. Brown hair hugged an angelic face and surrounded her captivating dark brown eyes. Her laughter recalled memories of a time before fate turned his life upside down. He wondered why fate hadn't brought them together sooner. When he was younger, and the number one stud in college. He'd asked himself the same question whenever he'd met other women after his accident. This time, though, he allowed the vision of Debbie to carry him through the dreams of what might have been, what could have been, and what should have been. Much too soon, the venom festering deep inside him returned, and he dismissed the fantasy.

Too late, the angel, he thought.

CHAPTER 31

Two days had passed and Scanlon was close to finishing with the pool at the Indian Shores motel when, as he expected, a punctual visitor strolled up to greet him.

"Good morning, Jerry."

"Good morning, Drew."

"I wasn't sure you'd stop by today. With the weather and all."

Scanlon smiled. "I figured I'd better keep to my schedule. No telling when I'll be able to come back."

A look of disappointment covered on the manager's face. "Oh. I'm sorry to hear that. Say, my shift is over, and I was wondering if you'd like to get some breakfast after you're done?"

"Can't, Drew. I've got three more jobs today." Scanlon paused long enough for the silence to become uncomfortable. "But I could come back tonight for a drink."

The young man's eyes glistened with anticipation. "I suppose I *could* slip away for a little while. If you came late enough, that is."

Scanlon kept to his work. "Around midnight okay?"

"Splendid! I'll see you then."

As the unsuspecting young man departed, Scanlon widened his smile.

CHAPTER 32

In no hurry to leave his apartment, Scanlon began a slow and easy drive to his rendezvous in Seminole. A ceiling of gray clouds and winds between twenty-five and thirty miles per hour had delivered rain from time to time, but would be of little consequence as far as he was concerned.

After he left St. Petersburg Beach, he drove through the community of South Pasadena to Park Street and turned left. The short, two-lane stretch of road at the beginning of the well-manicured and affluent neighborhood would see fewer vehicles due to the weather. A median of grass and young live oaks cohabiting with cabbage palms divided the road at 5th Avenue South. At 1ˢᵗ Avenue South, the roadway widened, and his speed increased a bit from there to Tyrone Boulevard and another left turn.

Once across the Seminole Bridge, he paid close attention to the speed limit and eased into the appropriate traffic lane. Prepared for the separation of the road as it arced to the left for Madeira Beach, he veered to the right toward his final destination.

Seminole Boulevard began the race with clusters of cars to Park Boulevard, completed in a matter of minutes and bringing yet another left turn. Less than a mile later, he arrived at the Raccoon Lake Apartments where Debbie lived. He slowed as he entered the complex to gain his bearings.

A well-displayed information sign indicated Building #4 was in the rear of the complex. He proceeded without difficulty to the structure that faced Old Oakhurst Road, but was a bit disappointed when no parking spaces in front of his destination were available. A short walk wouldn't punish his leg, but wouldn't help it, either.

As he neared the building, he noticed a curtain move in the window of the apartment on the right. A belief his date had been eagerly awaiting him filled his insides with a warm, pleasurable feeling. He entered the small lobby, paused to look around, and determined the layout of the units. The location of Debbie's apartment had already been established.

Two apartments, one in front of the other, were numbered one and three. Apartment number two, Debbie's residence, was located on the right. The door to apartment number four was partially hidden by a staircase that rose up to the second floor.

"Let's see who's behind door number two, shall we?" he whispered and gently rapped three times. "One Mississippi, two Mississippi..."

The door swung open and a smiling Debbie appeared.

"Hello, Jeff."

She was radiant and much prettier than he remembered in a brighter light. A bewitching smile magnified the delicate glow in her eyes.

"Hello, Debbie."

"Won't you come in? I was thinking we might relax and have a drink before dinner."

He glanced at his watch. "That sounds nice, but I probably should have mentioned our reservation is for eight o'clock. We have about twenty minutes to get there."

"No problem. Let me get my things." She returned in a few seconds wearing a look of uncertainty. "Do you think I'm dressed too casual for Devin's?"

Scanlon checked out her turquoise tank top, skinny blue jeans, and white leather sandals then nodded his approval.

"Debbie, this is Florida and its summer. Trust me. You look fine."

"You're right. To heck with them if they can't take a joke."

He followed her into the lobby, and they left the building. "Debbie, I hope you don't mind riding in a truck."

"I love trucks."

"I'm glad. I should have mentioned it."

He acted the gentleman and opened the door for her. When he'd joined her in the cab, he fired up the truck, backed out of the parking space, and pulled out onto Old Oakhurst Road.

"So how was your day?" he asked.

"Fine. Well, not really. I'm glad to be here and not at work. I think I told you I'm a legal assistant. Life in the office has been tense lately. We're handling some big cases and time is running short." Debbie sighed. "Oh, I don't want to bore you with all that." She lowered her head before turning to him. "Jeff, it's none of my business, but I noticed you kind of limp a little. Do you mind telling me what happened?"

He glanced at her out of the corner of his eye. "Football injury while I was in college."

"You played football?"

"For South Florida. I was a defensive back. I had a shot at the pros until I got hurt."

"Wait a minute! You're *that* Jeff Scanlon? I've seen you play. My boyfriend at the time took me to a few of your games."

"You like football?"

"I love football. I'm a big fan of the Bulls. That's why I remembered your name."

Scanlon felt the cold chill of uneasiness. "Small world, huh?"

"I don't believe it."

They left Old Oakhurst Road and their travel time on Duhme Road was brief, but enough for plenty of laughter and conversation until they came to the Tom Stuart Causeway and Madeira Beach. Once they were over the bridge, they continued on to Gulf Boulevard before making the turn south. Their pleasant exchange ended when John's Pass Village appeared on the left.

Scanlon made an easy right turn, and Devin's Seafood Saloon came into view. Lucky to find a parking space near the front door, he decided it was time to test his new acquaintance. She might prove to be the next person of interest after Drew Mitchell.

"Debbie, did you know John's Pass was formed by the Great Hurricane of 1848?"

"Yes, I did."

"Really? Well, then I must tell you I *am* impressed."

"I was born here, Jeff. Well, not *here*. In Dunedin actually, but I do know the history of the Pass."

"How about that? Two born and bred Floridians. We're a dying breed, you know."

"Yes, we are."

Saloon was not indicative of the upscale ambience Devin's exhibited. The specialty was Florida lobster, stone crab, and oysters from Apalachicola. On occasion, they flew in Maine lobsters to accommodate those who desired them and were not opposed to the inflated price.

The dining room was a veritable forest of Florida pine. Pinewood floors met with pinewood walls divided by red velvet wallpaper that surrounded spacious windows and continued up to the ceiling. Hung from four massive pinewood beams stretched overhead were an equal number of monstrous crystal chandeliers. Booths with red leather seats topped by etched glass mounted in pinewood lined the perimeter of the room. Two dozen tables covered the main floor, and a well-stocked bar sat to the right of the entrance. Devin's was quite a departure from the beachcomber atmosphere found in other nearby establishments.

The hostess greeted them with a smile, so Scanlon stepped up.

"Scanlon," he said. "I have an eight o'clock reservation. Might we have a booth on the beach side, please?"

"Certainly," she said.

She plucked two menus from the hostess station, led them to the middle of the row, and placed the menus on the table.

"Your server will be right with you."

Scanlon glanced through the window as he waited for Debbie to sit down. "I know the weather is lousy, but I like to look at the water."

"This is perfect," she said.

Once he was seated across from her, they began to peruse their menus.

"Good evening. I'm Gina and I'll be your server. Have you decided on your selections, or do you need more time?"

Scanlon looked at Debbie.

"Oh, I don't know," she said. "It all sounds delicious."

He smiled and looked up at Gina. "Give us a few minutes, please."

"Of course. May I get you something to drink?"

"A Sedona Light for me, please," Debbie said.

"Make it two."

Debbie looked away from the menu and gazed out the window. "Jeff, look."

A blanket of gray clouds courtesy of Hurricane Gloria lay above the horizon, a sun-brilliant shroud over the Gulf of Mexico. As the sun sank lower, its reflection painted the clouds like embers.

Debbie sighed. "It's so beautiful."

Gina returned with their drinks and took their orders.

A euphoric feeling wrapped itself around Scanlon. A relaxing exhilaration not brought on by alcohol or pills. Unusual after a hard day's work. He felt good again, and during the breaks in their conversation he stared deeply into Debbie's eyes. At one point he became curious why she kept shifting in her seat.

She finally slid out of the booth and stood up. A wide smile covered her face. "Excuse me, but the beer is starting to work."

Scanlon laughed as he watched her leave, and took a moment

to begin a slow, deliberate search of the restaurant.

Not too many people sat scattered about the dining room. No surprise since it was a weeknight. And the bad weather certainly didn't help. He noticed some elderly couples and a few families with children. Probably visitors on vacation. Three young men at the bar were laughing. Regulars by their looks. The two on the outside sat sideways and talked to the third and each other. The one in the middle did a great impersonation of someone engrossed in a ping-pong match and attempted to converse with both of them. Other couples here and there laughed and talked. One couple was getting very friendly. At the point where the bar curved and came to an end against the wall, Scanlon caught sight of an attractive brunette sitting alone. And she was staring at him.

At first, he was unmoved. She continued to stare. His mind raced to put a name with the face. Stymied, he looked away, still contemplating. He took a breath and glanced in her direction again. He grinned when he discovered she was still interested in him and acknowledged her fascination with a smile and a nod. The brunette never blinked as she leaned back in her bar chair. Then she winked at him.

Debbie returned at the same time their server brought his oysters. Gina noted his request for two more beers and left as he prepared to slurp down the first of a dozen.

"Do you use sauce and lemon juice?" Debbie asked.

"Just sauce. Lemon juice hides the taste."

She watched with great interest as he disposed of the mollusk.

"Would you like one?" he said.

"Just one."

Scanlon went after the largest.

"No! No! That one's too big." She pointed at the one nearest his left hand. "I'll take the little guy, there."

He speared the oyster with his small, dual tine fork. "The works?"

"Just sauce, please."

Scanlon gave it a generous swirl in the spicy condiment then guided it toward her. She took it in and immediately began to chew.

"You really *do* like oysters," he said. "Most people swallow them quickly, or make faces and don't eat them at all."

"It's the rubbery texture and the taste of shell they don't like. I don't mind, though. But I can't eat too many."

"Oh, and why is that?"

Debbie looked down at the table. "They make me horny."

Scanlon burst into laughter, and scooped up another oyster. "Then by all means."

Debbie raised her eyes and hands and laughed as she waved off the temptation.

When she turned to look at the dark Gulf waters, Scanlon cut a glance toward the bar. To his disappointment, the brunette was gone. He popped the oyster into his mouth and allowed the face of the mystery woman to slip from his mind.

"It's raining again," Debbie said.

Scanlon turned to discover a light veil of rain pelting the window in the early evening darkness.

CHAPTER 33

When they'd finished their supper, Debbie and Scanlon left the booth and took seats at the bar to continue their evening. Besides possessing beauty, wit, and intelligence, Debbie was a natural with conversation. Knowledgeable in a good many areas, she expressed curiosity about what she didn't know. Scanlon was stimulated by her charm. She revealed she had attended Hollins High School and St. Petersburg College before finishing her education at Florida State. Sports, especially college football and baseball, were high on her list of activities to watch while tennis, camping, and canoeing topped the list of those in which she participated.

"I love to go camping, but not at a campground with RV's and trailers," she said. "I like to go deep into the woods and rough it."

Intrigued, Scanlon speculated how someone who looked as though she would cry if she broke a fingernail could express a desire to trek into the wilderness. Was this an attempt to impress him, the former football player, or was she simply being honest? Once again, the question of why fate had waited so long to bring them together floated through his mind.

"Debbie, I'm having a hard time believing some guy hasn't stolen your heart by now."

Debbie's smile faded, along with the sparkle in her eyes. "Jeff... I seem to make bad choices when it comes to men. My friends tell me I see only what I want to see in them, and not what's really there. Hopeless romantic is what they call me."

"Well, don't change. You deserve the best."

Her smile returned, and she thanked him.

He couldn't remember the last time he'd seen a woman blush. When he glanced at his watch, shock surged through him.

"Wow! Look at the time."

"Is it late?"

"Eleven-thirty. I'd better get you home."

Debbie sighed. "Yes. Six-thirty comes awfully early."

They waited in front of the entrance for the latest downpour to let up. A continuous band of showers held them captive before it lessened and became a thin and misty shadow.

Scanlon took Debbie by the hand.

"It's now or never!" he shouted.

They hurried as best they could to his truck. When they pulled out of the parking lot and onto Gulf Boulevard, Debbie slid close to him and rested her head on his shoulder.

"This night went by way too fast for me," she said.

"Me, too."

Minutes passed as quickly as their evening together. Near the end of the ride, his leg began to hurt. Why, he didn't know. And he'd forgotten to bring his pills. He released a grateful sigh when he steered his truck off Old Oakhurst Road into the parking lot of the apartment complex. A space in front of her building was vacant. Another round of rain delayed their exit. They sat in silence and embraced the moment as well as each other. A long and lingering kiss soon followed.

"Jeff, I had a wonderful time," Debbie whispered.

"I hope we can do this again," he said.

"I'd like that." She looked deeply into his eyes. "I *really* would."

He smiled to display his happiness—and deception.

The rain eased up and allowed them time for an unhurried

stroll on the dampened sidewalk. A goodnight kiss in front of her door was the last he would see of her. Scanlon returned to his truck and started the engine. He drove to the front entrance, stopped, and tightened his grip on the steering wheel. Unlike the other women he'd been attracted to, Debbie would be difficult to forget. But he knew it would never work out between them. It couldn't. He was leaving town once his mission was completed.

With his mind still distracted by thoughts of Debbie, he didn't notice the car head out of the apartment complex shortly after he'd pulled into the street.

CHAPTER 34

Scanlon flipped on his high-beams and saw the glass-encased office of the Indian Shores motel light up when he veered into the parking lot. Aware he would get wet when he selected a parking space a fair distance away from the office, being nearer to the exit would make for a quicker escape. He noticed another vehicle roll past the motel and took a moment to watch it, relieved when the car turned into the condominium next door.

A light drizzle showered him as he ambled to the office, not the least bit concerned he was a few minutes late. He figured Drew Mitchell would be anxious to see him. He pulled the glass door open, stopped to wipe the rain from his face, and shuddered. "Boy, this is some night, huh?"

Mitchell took a deep breath and attempted a smile. "I was beginning to think you weren't coming."

Scanlon felt the night manager's eyes on him as he approached the counter. "I dozed off watching television. I hope you don't mind me being wet."

"Not at all." Mitchell's eyes never left him as he pulled a small bottle of Chablis and two plastic cups from under the counter. "How about a little taste of the grape to warm you up?"

"Good idea. But why don't we go somewhere less conspicuous."

"You mean outside? I'll get soaked."

Scanlon winked and motioned with his head. "Come on, Drew. It's only misting now."

Mitchell picked up the bottle and cups as he stepped from behind the counter and followed Scanlon out the door. Concrete walkways ran the length of the rooms on both sides of the pool before joining again and disappearing through an opening in a white, waist-high concrete wall. A lofty pair of Medjool date palms stood guard on either side of the walk inside the wall. Rows of variegated hibiscus bushes and leriope set in decorative red mulch signaled the end of the property.

Scanlon searched the area with a casual eye to make certain each room was dark, and became transfixed on the trees as they neared. He stopped and faced Mitchell between the two majestic palms, grasped the younger man's shoulders, then eased him up against one of the giant sentries.

Mitchell looked nervously in all directions. "Here? Why don't we wait until we get to the beach?"

Scanlon cupped Mitchell's face with both hands. "There's something I've been wanting to tell you."

The young man's face grew warm. Scanlon's touch hardened, and he slammed Mitchell's head into the trunk of the palm. Again! For the ever-lasting pain he'd endured. Again! For a football career destroyed. And again! For the disappointing life he'd been forced to live.

"Damn all of you out-of-towners to hell," he whispered.

With his chest rising and falling, Scanlon allowed the bloody pulp to slide through his hands and onto the ground. He came to realize the drizzle had turned to rain as he stood over the pitiful heap. The perfect cover to mount his escape.

"Sheriff's Office! Don't move!" a woman shouted.

Scanlon spun around as Jenny appeared from behind the row of rooms. With her Sig Sauer aimed and ready, she moved to within six feet of him and stopped. "Now put your hands on your head and face the other way!" she barked.

Scanlon did as he was ordered while his mind raced.

Jenny inched forward and rammed her automatic into his back. She ran her hand up and down his body, found no weapon, then retreated two steps. "Hands behind your back! Slowly!"

Scanlon lowered his arms, then spun around and clamped his hands over hers and the automatic. Jerking her arms high above her head, he fought to wrestle the weapon away from her. They struggled a few seconds, neither giving in to the other, until she kicked his left leg hard.

Scanlon cried out as his leg gave way, but didn't let go of her. As he wrenched her hands between them, they crashed to the sidewalk and the automatic roared. Both lay motionless in the next wave of rain. Chilly droplets showered his face as Scanlon slowly opened his eyes. The torrent of pain attacking his leg was merciless. He hoisted himself up onto one elbow and gazed at the unconscious woman beside him. A stream of blood flowed between them.

He reached out and grabbed the automatic that lay beside her, then forced himself to his feet. Favoring his throbbing leg as he stood over her, he wiped the rain from his eyes with the back of his hand and slowly raised the Sig Sauer.

"Hey!" someone yelled. "What the hell is going on out there?"

Scanlon looked up to discover a man and woman silhouetted in the doorway of the room on the very end. As quickly as he could, he turned and half-limped, half-ran around the side of the opposite building to the front of the motel. As he reached his truck, he stumbled, but was able to yank the door open, pull himself inside, and speed off down the rain-slick street.

CHAPTER 35

Four hours before Jan would attempt to swat her alarm clock to the floor, her phone ruined what little sleep she'd managed. She jumped awake and flailed the darkness in search of the infernal contraption. Seconds later, and somewhat cognizant, she picked up her phone.

"Jenny's been shot," the lieutenant said. "She's at Gulf Care Hospital on Walsingham Road in critical condition."

Jan dropped her phone and leapt from her bed. "Not again! Not again!" she kept shouting as she threw on her clothes.

Fear and anger played leapfrog inside her as she dashed to her car. She raced through the empty streets, the windshield wipers in constant battle with the hard-driving rain.

"What have you done, Jenny? What have you done?" Was it a bad decision? An impetuous moment? Or had Jenny's temper brought her down? And where had she gone? "Damn it, Jenny! Don't do this to me!" She slammed her fist against the steering wheel.

After a journey that felt too long in reaching an end, Jan sped into the parking lot of the Gulf Care Hospital and slid to a halt. She bolted from her car and sprinted across the shiny, puddle-strewn blacktop to the ER.

The lieutenant and two Indian Shores police officers stood waiting in the hall.

"Jenny's in bad shape, Jan," the lieutenant said. "She caught one in the gut, and she's lost a lot of blood."

"She and the night manager of the Indian Shores Motel were discovered around twelve-thirty this morning," one of the officers said. "The manager is dead. We think Detective Lester tried to stop his killer. Two witnesses said they saw a man running away."

"Did they give you a description of him?" Jan asked.

"Medium height was all they could tell us. Oh, and she must have injured him because he was favoring one of his legs."

"Which leg?"

"They didn't say."

The doors to an operating room opened and a silver-haired surgeon in green scrubs walked towards them. He made no attempt to disguise his grim expression.

"She's having a rough go of it," he said. "The next few hours will be critical." He searched the faces of the foursome. "I'm sorry."

After he left, Jan faced the lieutenant. "What the hell was she doing at a beach motel?"

"I was hoping you could tell me."

Jan tried to recall her last conversation with Jenny. Nothing helpful came to mind.

Waiting for an update began to wear on her and the lieutenant, and they prayed Jenny would pull through. In the pre-dawn hours, they received word she was in stable but guarded condition.

Jan had yet to come to terms with the tragic event. The memory of the death of her former partner, Seeward Sinclair, loomed over her like a merciless specter. And what had Jenny been doing at the motel in Indian Shores? Fatigue became too much ignore, so she decided a blast of hot, black coffee was necessary. As she stood in front of the coffee machine and rummaged through her pockets for the stack of small bills she always carried with her, an ER nurse walked up.

"Sergeant Larkin?"

"Yes."

The nurse looked in all directions. "I think you should know Detective Lester kept trying to say something when they brought her in." She looked around again. "I can't be certain, but it sounded like 'standing' or 'stand in.' I really couldn't tell."

Jan froze. An all too familiar name forced its way across her lips. "Could it have been Scanlon?"

"I can't be certain."

As she stormed out the doors to the ER, all the repressed rage over Seeward's death, and the realization Jenny might share the same fate, jetted to the surface. A glint of madness filled Jan's eyes. "Jenny, I'm going to kill him!" she whispered.

Large drops of rain pelted her and ran down her neck as she crossed the parking lot to her car.

CHAPTER 36

With time as his ally, Scanlon had packed most everything he owned into the bed of his truck, including the fine looking automatic he'd wrestled away from the sheriff's office bitch. He'd covered his belongings with a canvas tarp and was well into his escape by four a.m. Although his personal pledge of symbolic revenge remained unfulfilled, he felt he had no other choice but to run. Killing the cop had been a huge mistake. One he could live with, but the repercussions from the law enforcement community would be widespread and relentless. They wouldn't rest until they found the killer of one of their own.

Without provocation, the voice inside him spoke once more.

They know it's you.

A mountainous wave of apprehension rolled down his spine. The icy swell of fear stayed with him until he'd turned east on State Road 54.

When he reached U.S. 41, a smile creased his lips as one by one the faces of his victims appeared. The little girl. The old man. The accountant. The educators. The granddaughter. The widow. The motel manager. Not the thirteen victims he'd counted on, but an impressive score, nonetheless. He felt certain he could hide beneath the cover of obscurity at the cabin on Lake Bradley. Remain unobserved until time erased all traces of Jefferson Gerald Scanlon.

CHAPTER 37

Jan initiated a county-wide bulletin for Jefferson Gerald Scanlon once she returned to the office. She then turned her anger inward and rang an old acquaintance, a brilliant internet technician who knew how to get results. She needed to take a closer look at the pool cleaner's phone records. Ten minutes after she'd ended the call, she held the printed pages in her hand. The list was long, but mattered little as she noted each number with interest.

Going down the list, she got in touch with each party and inquired as to the person's relationship with Scanlon. The responses of the people who employed him were typical, but uninformative. Others knew him, but not very well. Some hadn't seen him in weeks. Call after call provided her with nothing to pinpoint the personality or tendencies of the man.

One name in particular caught Jan's attention. She thought it unusual it appeared only once. Scanlon had talked to most of the people multiple times, being they were his clients or old acquaintances from college. She picked up the receiver and dialed.

"Yellow!" a man answered.

"This is Detective Sergeant Jan Larkin of the Pinellas County Sheriff's Office. I'm trying to reach Charles Lyon."

"You got him."

"I'm calling in regard to a Jefferson Gerald Scanlon. Do you know him?"

"Jeff? Sure I do. We've been buds for a long time. Why? Did something happen to him?"

Another one who calls him Jeff, she thought. "How long have you known him?"

"Oh, let me see. Since high school, I guess."

"Do you know how he hurt his leg?"

"In a car accident. Some drunk tourist t-boned him and really screwed him up. It was while he was still in college. He was never able to play football again."

"He played football in college?"

"Yeah, in high school, too. He was the best player on our team. The accident ended his shot at playing pro ball. Is he all right?"

"Do you know what his major was in college?"

"I never asked him. He liked history in high school, though. He helped me get through it. That's a weird question. Why do you want to know?"

"Have you talked to him lately?"

"Not lately."

"When was the last time you talked to him?"

"I don't know. I'm not good with dates."

Jan glanced at the list. "Was it within the last month or so?"

"Yeah, that sounds about right."

"What did you discuss?"

"He was going on vacation and wanted to know if he could use my cabin."

"Your cabin?"

"Yeah. I got a cabin in Floral City."

Jan felt a strong surge of adrenaline. She got the address and directions to the cabin from Lyon and thanked him for his help.

Leaning back in her chair, she thought it odd only he and a few others on the list knew Scanlon as Jeff. In business, he was known as Jerry. And why did the name Jeff seem so familiar?

She sat up straight when the answer flew into her head. "Jeff is the name of the guy Jenny's friend met! Oh, Jenny, why didn't you tell me?"

Jan didn't hesitate to act on a decision she knew wouldn't set well with her superiors and picked up the phone to call the Citrus County Sheriff's Department. After her request to speak directly to the sheriff was permitted, she told him the entire story.

Reluctant at first, he finally offered his services, as well as those of his SWAT team, but with one stipulation. She must clear the operation with her superiors.

CHAPTER 38

The next morning Hurricane Gloria decided to turn north and unleashed her fury on the unfortunate residents of Apalachicola and Port St. Joe. The weather around the Tampa Bay area returned to normal and the broiler of summer. Blue skies and a steady breeze out of the southwest brought plenty of sweat for those who braved the outdoor life. The weather in Floral City was clear and hot as well.

Scanlon decided it was a good day for fishing and prepared to take the john boat out on Lake Bradley around 1 p.m. He planned to return at sunset.

Confident his stay at the cabin was no cause for concern, he kept up his affable demeanor with the few locals he'd met. To them, he was simply one more refugee from the city who felt the need to get away. Had they seen him before? They wouldn't remember—or care to remember.

He laughed as he set out in his launch and looked upon the deep, black water as a welcome friend. A friend who would serve as a protector from those who might come after him for all the unpleasantness he'd left behind. A friend like the automatic he kept stuffed in his waistband. Now was not the time to lower his guard.

CHAPTER 39

Jan requested her lieutenant consider the plan she'd devised. She'd received a stern reprimand for breaking the chain of command. After arguing with him for an hour, she sat at her desk and waited for him to consult with the sheriff. Whatever they decided was of no consequence. She'd made up her mind. With or without permission, she was going to Floral City. And with or without anyone's help, she was going to track down Jerry Scanlon. An hour passed before she received approval to go ahead with the operation.

Allowing for traffic, she would leave the office at three o'clock that afternoon with hopes of arriving in Floral City no later than six. There, she would meet with the SWAT team and go over every detail. If all went as designed, they would move on the cabin a little before sunset. Jan took a few moments to reflect upon everything that had transpired over the past few weeks. Her spirits were lifted a bit when she recalled the joke she and Crabby played on Jenny. Jenny. Despite all her efforts, Jan had grown close to the young detective. She would stop by to see her on the way out of town. Burn the image of her fallen friend and partner into her mind as a personal keepsake. Then she would go to Floral City and kill Jerry Scanlon.

CHAPTER 40

Jan arrived at the rendezvous point and met the SWAT team a little after six o'clock. Barbed wire fences lining both sides of the secluded dirt road south of Floral City seemed to go on forever. She was then introduced to each of the men and the two women who comprised the team. When she told the team about Jenny, all agreed no matter how the operation went down, Jan would get credit for the arrest. For all her years on the force, the veteran detective had never been part of a tactical operation, so she listened intently as the SWAT lieutenant began the briefing.

With a slow and deliberate delivery, he went over every detail of the assault: their approach through the live oaks on the east side of the cabin, the responsibilities of each team and team member, and their positioning around the perimeter. The lieutenant then focused on her and explained how they would go about taking down Scanlon—one way or the other. With the briefing concluded, they left as a group and headed in the direction of a two-lane road on the far side of their objective.

The caravan ride lasted longer than Jan would have liked, but when they arrived at the end of East Lake Bradley Road, she and the SWAT team left their vehicles and spread out in a wide, single line. Their long, thin shadows trailed their every step as they began the assault.

The sun was past setting and twilight beginning to fade when they crept into a dense forest of live oaks. Overhead, the massive limbs and leaves formed a natural canopy. Spanish moss clung to each trunk, dangled from the branches, or lay on the ground in clumps.

Jan's focus slipped as she envisioned Seeward Sinclair stalking Eddie Papalos on the grounds of the farmhouse, his only intention to kill the man. She considered every thought that may have entered his mind right up until the shots were fired. Could he have felt the same anger and rage for Papalos she now felt for Jerry Scanlon? Was it the desire to see justice served that drove him to the rural area outside of Brandon? The same desire which had driven her here. Whatever the reason didn't matter now. When she got the chance, she was going to kill him. A tree branch snapped under her foot and yanked her focus back to the group.

The distance to the cabin seemed farther than it appeared on the map. Humidity and nerves brought sweat and mosquitoes. Still wet and soft from days of rain, the carpet of grass beneath their feet silenced the approach of the team. Through the thin stand of trees in front of them, they could see the rustic dwelling.

The lieutenant signaled the squad on his left to cover the rear of the cabin, a task made easier by the presence of a pickup truck covered with a tarp as a barricade.

Jan recognized it at once. "That's Scanlon's truck," she whispered to the lieutenant.

The lieutenant then signaled the squad on his right to move to the front of the darkened cabin. In silence, the teams moved into position and waited. The antiquated building yielded no signs of life or sounds of movement. Two solid smashes from a battering ram toppled the aged wooden door, and the team members in front of Jan poured inside with their flashlight beams dancing in all directions.

The cabin was empty.

"Damn it!" she yelled.

The lieutenant frowned and ordered both teams to stand down.

A voice from the outside team suddenly crackled over their headsets.

"Boat approaching."

The team inside scrambled through the doorway and assumed positions along the front of cabin so as not to be seen from the lake. The team in the rear split up, with three members taking positions on the blind side of the truck. The rest of the squad moved into a stand of cypress trees clustered along the shore on the west side of the dock.

The sound of the boat's motor grew louder, then ceased, only the sound of water slapping against its hull. Darkness covered the grounds, but a cloudless, pale yellow sky provided the perfect backdrop.

The solitary silhouette in the boat stood up as it bumped against the dock. He tied it off, carefully climbed out, and walked toward them.

The lieutenant didn't wait for him to reach the shore. "Citrus County Sheriff's Department! Don't move!"

The figure stopped walking, stepped back, then jumped into the pitch-black water as two red-orange flashes from the pistol he wielded revealed his position. The hollow reports ricocheted through the trees and rolled out over the lake.

"Hold your fire!" the lieutenant yelled.

Sloshing sounds announced Jerry Scanlon's attempt to escape as he struggled through the water toward the cypress trees.

Jan lost sight of him in the shadows beneath the dock, but held her position.

"He's almost on us," whispered the squad leader of the team concealed in the cypress trees.

The lieutenant turned to Jan and nodded.

She leaned forward and strained to get a better look.

A low, guttural growl, then a roar sounded above Scanlon's watery thrashings before he screamed.

The team around the cabin dashed toward the lake as flashlights in the cypress trees lit up the darkness.

"Over here!" someone shouted.

Maneuvering along the water's edge toward the concentration of light, Jan and the team found Scanlon lying on his back in the shallows, his arms wrapped tightly around a pair of Cypress knees.

"Gator got him," the baby-faced squad leader said. "He was comin' right to us.

We were just about to grab him when this big ol' gator jumped up and tore his leg clean off."

The lieutenant looked up from the mangled body. "We need a medic over here!"

"He's dead, Lieutenant," Baby Face said.

Jan felt the warmth of relief as well as the weight of fatigue as she shoved her automatic into its holster. "The gator got your good leg," she said.

"What was that, Sergeant?" the lieutenant asked.

"Nothing, sir. Just a cruel joke directed at a cruel man."

CHAPTER 41

Jan released a long, quiet sigh as she watched Doctor Donna Suarez finish her notes. She knew the doctor had worked with many law enforcement officers and helped them come to terms with various forms of occupational burnout an oblivious public would never understand. There was no hiding the fact Jan was dealing with a classic case of work-related stress. An attempt to deceive someone with so many years in the field of psychology was an exercise in futility.

Suarez leaned back in her chair. "Jan, you've made a great deal of progress since you've been to see me. I'm pleased with the results, and I hope you are as well."

Jan nodded.

"But I still believe there's something you're not telling me."

That's right, Jan thought. *And it's something neither you nor anyone else will ever know.* She shifted in her chair and shrugged. "I don't know what else there is to tell, Doctor."

The psychiatrist smiled. "How's Jenny?"

"She's recovering nicely. She admitted she's having nightmares, but I'm sure she'll get over them and be back to work soon."

"Did she tell you about the nightmares?"

"I didn't push her."

"Did she tell you anything else?"

"Not that I recall."

The doctor studied her patient.

Jan lowered her head. "Jenny's thinking about leaving the force. I'd hate to see her go. She's a good cop... and a good partner. I can't imagine her doing anything else."

"Jan, fear affects people differently. She may reconsider leaving after she's fully recovered." Suarez paused. "Is that the only reason you'd hate to see her go?"

"Doctor, I... Losing Seeward was bad enough. If Jenny left... well... I'd get over it, of course, but the thought of having to train another partner...I don't know."

"Do you think about Seeward a lot?"

"Not a lot. I don't usually have the time."

"How long has it been since you've taken a vacation?"

"Three or four months, maybe."

"Right after Seeward was shot?"

"Yes."

"Why didn't you come to me then?"

"I didn't feel the need. The time off did me good. Being away from the job did the trick."

Suarez nodded. Her eyes never left the veteran detective. "Jan, I'm going to recommend you take a two-month leave of absence. I believe that will be a sufficient amount of time. When you return, we can re-evaluate your situation."

A leave of absence hadn't occurred to Jan. "Two months? But, Doctor, I..."

She stopped when she realized her protest would be in vain.

Crabby's offer to roam the Gulf of Mexico in his boat for relaxation, closure, and, most of all, peace of mind had worked wonders in the past. A leave of absence, though, was an entirely different matter.

"I guess you know what's best, Doctor. I don't suppose I have a choice."

"Believe me, Jan, you can use the rest."

Jan pictured the old salt behind the wheel of his trawler and smiled.

"Why are you smiling?"

"Doctor, while I'm resting, I think I'm going to do a little fishing."

SHADOW OF DECEIT

CHAPTER 1

Two dolphins raced along the port side of the twenty-six-foot Outer Reef trawler, slicing through the Gulf waters off the coast of central Florida. Spouting air while cavorting and playing, they were making the most of their time together. In the final days of her two-month leave of absence, Jan had given a lot of thought to the next chapter of her life. Although she hadn't made an official announcement, she planned to request a transfer out of the Homicide Division of the Pinellas County Sheriff's Office. Twelve years of tracking down killers had taken its toll. The murder of her former partner, Seeward Sinclair, followed by the near-death of her current partner, Jenny Lester, had jarred her emotionally, prompting her decision. The investigation of those who murdered took a special kind of person. She had been that type of person for a long time—too long a time—and a change was needed.

Through the windshield of the trawler christened *Serafina*, Jan watched the graceful mammals enjoy their race with the boat. "Look at them, Crabby!" she yelled above the noise of the engines. "They seem so happy and carefree."

Morton "Crabby" Phillips, her newfound friend and confidant, let loose his usual snort. "Course they do, Cap'um. They's probably knowed each other fer quite a spell and enjoys bein' together."

Jan lifted her eyes to the cobalt sky and the wispy cirrus

clouds hanging overhead.

She closed them as a smile brightened her face.

During her last murder case, she and Crabby had spent a delightful evening at their favorite watering hole, the Spinnaker Bar and Grill in Treasure Island. The old salt had suggested she needed a companion as a pleasant diversion from her fast-track life. She'd laughed at the notion, giving him plenty of reasons why life with a cop could be difficult. Before he could argue, she had changed the subject, unwilling to deal with the emptiness she fought so hard to repress. From time to time, his words ambushed her like the ill-received advice from her father and the sorrowful memories she held of Ken and their failed marriage. She had vowed to never again let anyone interfere with her professional life.

A warm afternoon breeze stoked by an early autumn sun danced across her face as they neared the Hurricane Watch Marina. As the trawler was directed into the mouth of John's Pass by its strong currents, she squinted to scan the bridge joining Treasure Island and Madeira Beach.

Crabby steered them in a slow angle starboard on a path toward the marina. "Jan, look! There's somebuddy a-waitin' fer us on the dock!" he bellowed.

Bringing a hand to her forehead to block the sun's glare, Jan spied a lone female looking in their direction. Even with the distance between them, she determined the woman was young and acting very anxious. In the ensuing moments, she recognized her.

"Crabby, it's Jenny!"

As she waved her arms, Jenny's smile was as blinding as the sun. "Jan! Crabby! Hey! Hey!"

"Hey, Jenny!" Jan hollered back.

Crabby lifted a salute as he piloted the trawler nearer the dock.

The boat had barely bumped into the pilings when Jan leapt off and threw her arms around her friend and partner. "Oh,

Jenny, it's so good to see you."

"I missed you, too, Jan. You have no idea how much I've missed you."

They both turned back to the trawler when they heard Crabby's gravelly voice.

"Do ya mind heppin' me tie 'er off, Jan? I'd like ta get in on some o' that huggin', too, ya know."

Jenny laughed as he tossed the bowline, and Jan wrapped it around a dock cleat. Once the aft line was secured, the old mariner hopped onto the dock and clasped his calloused hands around Jenny's shoulders. He paused to gaze into her sparkling blue eyes. "Would ya mind a ole man given' ya a welcome back hug?"

Jenny was quick to embrace him. "Oh, Crabby. I thought I was never going to see you again." Overcome by emotion, a tear trailed slowly down her cheek.

"I know how ya feels, darlin'. I thought fer sure we was gonna lose ya." Crabby held her a few seconds longer. "Glad ya didn't let that happen." He eased her back and smiled, his yellow-tinged teeth showing through his snowy-white mustache and beard.

Jan decided the time was right to lighten the moment. "Hey, Jenny, what say we go to the Spinnaker and have a few beers? Crabby's buying."

"Now that's a dang good idea, Jan," Crabby said. "Wait a minute! I'm doin' what?"

Jenny laughed and hugged him again. "I'm all for it. Besides, I have something wonderful to tell both of you."

Jan took her by the arm, and they walked along the dock toward the boat storage building. Crabby followed close behind them, scratching his head through his battered blue captain's hat.

CHAPTER 2

The trio entered the Spinnaker Bar and Grill through the weathered wooden door and were greeted by a host of laughter and loud conversation. The afternoon crowd was larger than Jan had anticipated. Luck was on their side when two people in the last booth in a row of five got up to leave. Without hesitation, they hurried to claim it.

"Poseidon must be smilin' on us," Crabby said.

He waited for Jan to slide into the booth then eased in next to her. Jenny took a seat across from them.

Jan cut a glance at her partner, then turned to Crabby. "Don't get too comfy, you old sea dog. We're thirsty."

Crabby eyed her for a second. "Oh, all right. I'll gets the beer." He shifted his gaze to Jenny. "And you is partial to Sedona Light, right, darlin' Jenny?"

"You remembered."

He got up to leave.

"Hey! What about me?" Jan said.

Crabby waved her off. "I already knows what you want."

The women looked at each other and laughed.

"I can't wait until you get back to work," Jenny said. "I mean, I've only been back a few weeks myself, but it hasn't been the same around the office without you. Even some of the guys said so. Just knowing you'll be sitting at your desk again makes me feel..." She stopped when she noticed the uneasy

212

expression on Jan's face. "Did I say something wrong?"

Jan lowered her eyes. "Jenny, this is hard for me to say. I've had time to do a lot of thinking, and I, well, I've decided to transfer out of Homicide."

Jenny's smile vanished.

"I was going to tell you, but I was waiting for the right time."

"You're not joking, are you? You're really going to leave Homicide?"

Jan released a sigh and nodded her head.

"Why?"

"Because I'm tired of seeing murder victims. And I'm tired of playing cat-and-mouse with their killers. It gets tougher all the time. And, to be perfectly honest, I'm damn sick and tired of worrying about losing another partner."

Before Jenny could answer, Crabby returned with their drinks.

"Here ya go, ladies. Brews alla 'round." He set the bottle of Sedona Light in front of Jenny and pushed a frosty mug over to Jan. "I'll tell ya what. Sometimes that Hank can sure come up with some funny stories. He was jus' tellin' me 'bout the time these two fellers was a-sittin' at the bar, an'..." He noticed his friends were staring at their drinks as he sat down. He paused before taking a healthy pull of beer. "One o' ya wants ta tell me what's goin' on 'ere?"

Neither Jan nor Jenny answered or would look at him.

He took another long draw of beer and waited.

"I'm transferring out of Homicide," Jan said.

Crabby wrapped both hands around his mug. "Can't see why ya'd wanna go an' do that, Jan. Yer too good at it."

"Damn straight!" Jenny blurted out.

Her swearing surprised her friends. They looked at her a second then burst into laughter.

Jenny's face reddened. "Well, it's true."

Jan turned to Crabby. "Damn straight I am!"

Jenny joined in the laughter. "Okay, okay, that's enough. Anyway, I have some wonderful news I'd like to share with you." She took a deep breath. "I met a guy recently. His name is Rick Lennon and, uh...we've been seeing a lot of each other."

"When did this happen?" Jan said.

"About three weeks ago, I guess."

"Where did you meet him?"

"At the grocery store. Can you believe it? We were both heading for the same checkout line, not paying attention, and ran our shopping carts into each other."

"He didn't hurt ya none, did 'e?" Crabby said.

"No, we laughed about it. And then we started talking."

"Jenny, I've seen that movie," Jan said. "Are you sure he didn't run into you on purpose?"

"No, Jan, he apologized several times. He walked me to my car and put my groceries in the back seat for me. A real gentleman. We agreed to meet for lunch a couple of days later, and after that, we started seeing each other. I really like him."

Jan and Crabby sat poised and waited for her to continue.

"And?" Jan said.

"And I wanted you two to be the first to know."

"Is that it?"

Jenny smiled and shrugged.

CHAPTER 3

On her first day back in the office, Jan received a hardy welcome from her fellow detectives. The lieutenant and the captain stopped by as well. She hid the fact she was still feeling edgy and anxious. Being away from the job for two months was part of the problem. The decision to leave Homicide was the biggest hitch. When she saw Jenny was already at her desk, the butterflies disappeared.

Their night at the Spinnaker with Crabby, and her partner's announcement of a new acquaintance, was still very fresh in her mind. Her friend had smiled every time she mentioned him. A growing uneasiness had tempered happiness for Jenny. The young detective's confession of recurrent bad luck with relationships was a definite cause for concern. And what seemed to Jan to be an immediate acceptance of this stranger bothered her even more. Still, she hoped she might be wrong and the relationship would work out for her friend.

Jan went straight to her desk and sat down, still somewhat off-balance, still uncertain she wanted to jump back into the dark world of a homicide detective. From out of the corner of her eye, she saw a steaming mug of coffee and a man's hand. She looked up to discover both belonged to Detective Ray Poppel.

A wide smile covered his face as he set down the mug. "Hello. In case you've forgotten, my name is Ray. I wasn't sure how you took your coffee, so I left it black."

"Hello yourself, smartass. And you know I take my coffee black."

Poppel's laughter was full and hearty. "Good to have you back, Sergeant."

Jan picked up the mug and blew across the top. She took a sip and slowly swallowed. "Ah, yes," she said. "It's as awful as I remembered."

Poppel laughed again.

Jan glanced at Jenny and saw her smiling. "So what's up with you, Detective?"

"Me? Oh, nothing at all, Sergeant. I was just about to—"

The telephone cut short her reply.

A cold, sharp flood of adrenaline shot down Jan's spine. The phone rang a second time, resulting in a stare down between the two detectives. Jan fought the nervousness building inside her. A reluctance to enter into another encounter with some antisocial misfit so soon. The third ring never sounded.

Jenny gave her an exasperated look as she took the call. She nodded a couple of times and jotted down the information before replacing the receiver. "Hidden Rocks Beach, Jan. Some fellow named Munyer was found dead in a beach chair." She got to her feet and started to leave.

Jan felt a constriction she'd never experienced before. She couldn't get up from her chair. Jenny's account of what had transpired between her and the serial killer Jerry Scanlon that ill-fated night in Indian Shores two months ago poured into her mind. A fuzzy black-and-white image of the young detective lying on a rain-soaked sidewalk with the life running out of her held Jan captive. An unwillingness to view another tragedy involving her partner tightly bound her.

Jenny was nearing the office door when she realized she was alone. She waited a moment before turning around. "Come on, Jan, let's go."

Jan didn't move. Something deep inside her signaled a catastrophe yet to come.

"Jan!"

The veteran detective shook her head. "Yeah! Okay, let's go." She forced herself to her feet, took a deep breath, and followed her partner out the door.

CHAPTER 4

Hidden Rocks Beach was one of many small communities nestled along Florida's west coast. Unlike others its size, the town had seen more trouble than most in recent years. Corrupt town officials and murders were the latest black marks on the peaceful haven of natives, retirees, and vacationers. Another murder would thrust the town back into the regional limelight.

Jan was still pondering her aversion to the phone call. She felt unprepared when she entered the office and wondered if her extended absence triggered a reluctance to answer the phone. She'd never hesitated to act when called upon before. Her odd response may be one more reason to follow through with the transfer.

As she steered their gray sedan down Seminole Boulevard, Jenny kept glancing at her partner. "Kind of tough jumping back into the trenches, huh?"

"What? Oh. Yeah."

"Jan, are you sure you're all right?"

"Of course. Like you said, it's tough jumping back into the trenches. Nothing to worry about, though."

"I can't imagine how you must feel. Two months is a long time."

"It sure felt a lot longer I can tell you."

"Is there something on your mind?"

Jan hesitated as she peered out the window. "Jenny, you're

right. You can't imagine what I'm feeling. You have no idea of what was going through my mind when I was told you might die. I kind of went crazy. I felt like I'd let you down. And all I wanted to do was kill Jerry Scanlon."

"Jan, it wasn't your fault. I was worried about my friend, Debbie. I did a real stupid thing by going after Scanlon alone. I made a mistake. And I promise you it won't happen again."

A smile spread across Jan's face as she turned to her. "Thanks, Jenny. And if I stay I promise I won't ever leave you out of the loop again either."

They pulled into the parking lot at Seahorse Park after a three-minute ride along Gulf Boulevard. An ambulance crew and three uniformed deputies were waiting for them by the concrete wall lining the perimeter. When Jan and Jenny walked onto the beach, they saw one of the dozen chaise lounges was cordoned off.

Forensics technician Judy Walker stood outside the yellow and black crime scene tape with more deputies, some of her forensics team, and the usual assortment of gawkers who had gathered a short distance away. She took one last picture as the detectives approached.

Jenny moved under the tape and leaned over the victim. "Who found him, Judy?"

Walker nodded toward the small group of people. "The blonde wearing the pink visor. She rents the chairs."

"I'll go talk to her."

Walker's expression suggested she was a bit surprised Jenny would assume control of the investigation.

"She's a good cop, isn't she?" Jan said.

"Yeah. A real take charge kind of person. Makes your life a lot easier, I bet." Walker lifted the tape for her. "Welcome back, Jan." She began to take more pictures.

Jan donned a pair of plastic gloves and moved closer to the victim who wore red swim trunks and nothing else. He appeared to be very much at peace stretched out in the chair.

There were no signs of a struggle and no weapon lying nearby.

"He looks like he's asleep," Jan said as she leaned forward. "Severe bruising around his throat, though. Judy, besides being strangled, I think his neck's been broken. What's your take?"

"At first glance, I'd agree with you."

Jan scanned the immediate area around the beach chair. "Same old story, Judy. There are a thousand little dents in the sand and not one clean footprint to help us."

"I saw a couple of partials we might be able to lift. Maybe they can tell us something."

"Find anything, Jan?" Jenny said from outside the tape.

"Looks like he's been strangled and had his neck broken. No other visible wounds."

"Veronica Royer, the woman who rents the chairs, said his name is Murphy Munyer. He's retired and has been a regular visitor here for the last few years."

Jan searched both pockets of the victim's swim trunks but found no identification.

"Royer said Munyer walked the beach almost every day," Jenny said. "She has no idea where he's from."

"Well, let's talk to some of these folks and see if anyone knows him. Then we'll get the deputies to help us check the houses and condos."

Another difficult case had been dropped in their laps. Nothing had changed in Jan's time away. She was still considering the transfer when a stop at a red light allowed her partner to face her.

"Jan, I really need to know where you stand. I mean, it's only fair if you're sticking to the idea of leaving."

Jan was caught off guard by Jenny's directness. At any other time she would have been insulted. But more than once she had declared if she was ever unable to do her job, she would quit. Not giving a case her fullest attention was not doing her job.

"I can't give you an answer right now because I honestly don't know."

"Well, make up your mind soon, Sergeant. I don't want to go into this case half-assed if you're going to be distracted."

Jenny's aggressive behavior irritated Jan, but she knew her partner was right. There was no sense in moving forward if she harbored doubts about remaining in Homicide.

CHAPTER 5

Jenny went straight to her computer to do a search of Murphy Munyer.

Relieved her partner had not pressed her further, Jan stood by her desk, lost and off balance. Besides the other problems she was facing, the thought of abandoning Jenny had kept her from making her request for reassignment official. Crabby and Jenny were right, though. She *was* good at tracking down murderers. Maybe the hiatus and too much time to think had prompted the idea of making a change. Or maybe, as Dr. Suarez had suggested, fear affected people differently.

"Why does life have to be so complicated?" she mumbled.

The telephone saved her from further mental anguish. Jenny was preoccupied with gathering information, so she took the call. The conversation with Judy Walker was brief. An unexpected light-hearted feeling came over Jan. She smiled to herself, sat down, and pretended to be busy. She knew Jenny's curious nature would be aroused very soon.

"So what was that all about?" Jenny asked, her eyes never leaving her computer monitor.

"What?"

"The phone call."

"Oh. It was Judy Walker with an update."

"And?"

"And she found the victim's wallet buried in the sand a few

feet from the chair. Seems he's from Michigan. A cop in Detroit." She heard Jenny stop typing, then begin another round of clacking away on the computer keyboard.

"Here it is," Jenny said. "Murphy Munyer. Detroit P.D. A retired Vice lieutenant, and he'd...Oh, wow!"

"Oh, wow what?" Jan asked.

"He received about every commendation imaginable. A legend in the department. Uh-oh. He was investigated by Internal Affairs for alleged association with organized crime. His new address is, make that *was*, a condo five blocks from where he was discovered."

"I guess we should have widened our search a bit more. We'd better go over there and take a look around his place."

Jenny peered over the top of the monitor. "Are you sure, Jan?"

Jan got to her feet. "Let's go, partner."

"Are you *really* sure?"

Jan wasn't sure, but knew the only way to find the answer was to keep doing her job.

CHAPTER 6

The Sea Anemone Condominiums were upscale beachfront residences. A huge leap up the food chain for a vice detective from Detroit. Even a retired lieutenant.

Hoping Jenny could put aside the belief she wasn't totally committed to keeping her job, Jan did her best to proceed as if nothing had changed.

With no building manager to be found, the detectives approached the first resident they met. The friendly, silver-haired gentleman directed them to the unit belonging to William P. Marchant, president of the condominium association. The initial encounter was not encouraging.

"I hope your investigation won't be too much of an inconvenience," Marchant said. "We're a close-knit family here and we're not fond of unnecessary disruptions."

"We just need to search his condo," Jenny said. "No one will even know we're here unless *someone* tells them."

Marchant frowned. "I'll attempt to locate Johnny for you. Until then, please do your best to be discreet."

"And Johnny would be the building manager?"

Marchant ignored her and raised his phone to his ear.

Within minutes, they met with Johnny Henson, the building manager. After identifying themselves, they were let inside the home of Murphy Munyer.

Jenny pulled out her phone. "I'll bet seeing Forensics arrive will really chafe Marchant's ass."

Jan smiled and shook her head.

The former Detroit detective's suspected connection to organized crime was reinforced when they caught sight of an expensive bamboo sofa with black leather cushions. Four lounge chairs the same color and two Tiffany floor lamps sat atop a wall-to-wall charcoal carpet in the living room. His bedroom furnishings matched the elegance of the living room, and a closet with a trio of mirrored sliding doors revealed a surplus of luxurious apparel.

"Would you look at these suits," Jenny said. "Top of the line and custom tailored, I bet. And look at all the shirts and Italian leather shoes. Highly unusual for a cop. No wonder this guy was suspected of being dirty."

Jan was busy looking over Munyer's king-sized bed with silk sheets and crushed velvet bedspread. A burning sensation grew inside her. She despised cops who were opportunists, the kind who walked around with their hands out, and then hid behind their badges. "No doubt about it, Jenny. This guy was dirty. I hate that!"

"So do I. And I want to know who killed him and why."

"Judy Walker said nothing appeared to be missing from his wallet, so I think we can rule out robbery."

"This place doesn't look like it's been tossed. Could be someone just wanted Munyer dead."

Jan leveled a steely glare at Jenny. "We need to find out more about this guy. His relatives, who his friends are, and who he might have been working for after leaving the force. Maybe then we'll have a better idea of why he was killed."

"Does that mean you're staying?"

Jan ignored the question. "I've got a feeling there's more going on here than just murder." She turned and walked out of the bedroom.

"Welcome back, Sergeant," Jenny whispered.

CHAPTER 7

Once they'd finished rummaging through Munyer's home and were back at the office, a closer examination of the allegations against him turned up some very unpleasant results. Evidence implicating certain persons of interest disappeared before their court dates. In two separate cases, the state's star witnesses had died. The man was killed in a traffic accident. The woman, aged thirty-seven, had succumbed to a heart attack. A surveillance camera had even caught Munyer meeting with the lawyer of a known Detroit crime family, but no proof of collusion could ever be established.

Jan glanced at Jenny and saw her partner focused on her computer monitor.

She then struck a familiar pose in front of the clue board with her left arm laying across her stomach in support of her right, hand pulling gently on her chin. Her attention drawn to what little evidence they'd obtained. She was not happy.

"Jan, do you think the Detroit crime family Munyer was alleged to have been connected to sent someone to take him out?" Jenny said.

The senior detective heard her partner, but didn't budge, locked into her own theories why such a highly decorated cop, a lieutenant at retirement, had elected to join the opposition. Money always topped the list, and, by the looks of his condo, might be the primary reason. But she wondered why anyone would bother to come after him since he was no longer in the game. Unless he had something to hide. There was no evidence pressure from the law might force him to reveal the source of his lavish lifestyle. And nothing to indicate he'd ever crossed anyone important. Then again, maybe he had.

"Jan!" Jenny called out.

"What?"

"Do you think the Detroit syndicate had Munyer offed?"

"It's possible. But I'm not all in on it." Jan turned and faced her. "Unless the FBI or another agency was pressuring him to turn state's evidence against someone in the family."

"Do you think he might have hooked up with some bad guys down here? I mean, the man drove a brand new Porsche 911 GT 3, and they ain't cheap."

"Could be. Greed has always been a strong motivation. How much did he have in his savings account?"

Jenny's eyes darted back to the monitor. "Four hundred thirty-two thousand, six hundred thirty-nine dollars and twenty-three cents."

"Not to mention how much he may have stashed away in some off-shore accounts."

"You know, his condo was really clean. Almost immaculate. Seems like there would have been something to point to his dealings with the dark side. I mean, nobody's perfect."

"Well, think about it, Jenny. By all appearances he was dirty, but the Michigan State Attorney's Office couldn't come up with a charge that would stick. He left the department as a lieutenant *and* with his pension. He came down here with a nice little nest egg, settled into a luxurious seaside condo, and nothing about him reeked of impropriety. Smart and careful. That's how I see him."

Jenny's blue eyes settled on her partner.

Jan threw up her hands. "All right! We'll go back and take another look."

Moments like this were frustrating and another reason Jan

felt like she wanted to transfer out of Homicide. But the tough cases were always irritating.

CHAPTER 8

The ensuing hour found Jan and Jenny still searching of the retired detective's residence. And still empty-handed. They'd checked every conceivable hiding place, and each time had come away with nothing but frustration for their effort.

A painting in the living room had caught Jan's eye during their first visit. Drawn to it again, she stopped to admire the work of art. "Jenny, I don't think there's any hard evidence here to implicate Munyer being dirty."

Jenny ignored her and continued to scan a shelf filled with throwback vinyl LPs and once popular CDs. A Dual turntable, an Onkyo CD player and sound system filled the shelf below them.

Jan was still captivated by the Gauguin-like painting of a small sailboat heading towards a much larger tropical sunset. Oranges, reds, and yellows dominated the canvas with only the dark brown of the boat and blue-green of the water standing out in contrast. "Jenny, the boat in this painting is named after you. *Jennie L*, it says."

"That's funny."

"Yeah. Except its spelled J-E-N-N-I-E."

"Wait! It has *my* name on it?" Jenny began searching the LPs, but didn't find the one she wanted. Next, she filed through the CDs, focusing on the name of each artist.

A second later she spun around.

"Jan, I found a CD by Jennifer Liarta called *Chasing The Sunset*." She walked it over to her partner. "The picture on the front is exactly like this painting."

"One of your favorites I suppose."

"I like her, but only old people buy CDs anymore."

"Well, I guess Munyer liked her enough to have someone do a painting." Jan was about to turn away when something about the shape of the sun in the painting caught her eye. The orb was perfectly round and sat halfway beneath the water, out of context with the freehand style of the artist. "Now that's odd."

"You're telling me. Jennifer Liarta never made an album or CD called *Chasing The Sunset*.

"Are you sure?"

"Positive. And this disc holder is empty."

Jan kept staring at the painting. "There's something wrong here, too." She removed the painting from the wall and turned it over.

The back of the frame was lined with brown wrapping paper. Starting in the lower left corner, she pushed down with her thumb until it tore open. The paper backing separated easily from the frame and revealed a CD secured to the back of the canvas with adhesive tape. Once she removed the disc, Jan flipped it over to look at the hidden side.

The disc was the same color as the sun in the painting. At first glance, it easily blended in with the seascape.

She handed Jenny the disc. "Put this in the CD player and let's have a listen."

Jenny loaded the player, and much to the surprise of both detectives, not a sound was heard.

"It must be a data disc, Jan. We need to get back to the office."

They hurried to their car and drove back to the office. Jan was as eager as Jenny to find out what information was hidden on the disc.

CHAPTER 9

Jan walked to her partner's desk after hearing Jenny slam her fist.

"Damn it! It's all numbers and letters," Jenny bellowed, her blue eyes narrowed as she stared at her computer monitor.

Jan focused on the information. "Looks like something a millennial nerd might have devised."

"I can't make jack shit out of this mess."

In five separated rows, a collection of numbers and letters made up the mystery on the computer disc.

The first row read: 974241—970114—41178—8707—12—34700—971910—FGHEIKEE. The different combinations of the next four rows, while similar to the first, only compounded the enigma.

"How the *hell* are we supposed to figure this out?" Jenny grumbled.

Jan rested a hand on her partner's shoulder. "I know an instructor at the University of South Florida who's an encryption expert. I'll give him a call and see if he can help us." She paused a moment. "Jenny, just out of curiosity, when did you start swearing so much?"

The young detective sat back and folded her arms. "Ever since I got shot in the gut."

CHAPTER 10

The following morning, Jan and Jenny were standing at the furthest end of Lake Seminole Park. A fisherman had discovered a body in an abandoned john boat. He admitted he didn't pay much attention to the boat at first until he saw it wasn't anchored to the shore. He pulled alongside and have a look.

"The victim is Nathan Parker, fifty-five, big shot land developer," Jenny said. "Lives in Belleair, probably in a mansion. Probably divorced after his wife caught him screwing around. He's CEO of Parker, Bittner and Crosland Developers."

"You came up with all that from his driver's license?" Jan asked.

"His driver's license, business card, and conjecture."

"Well, stick to the facts, Detective. Call his office and see if you can find out the reason for him being here." Jan turned to Forensics Technician Judy Walker. "Talk to me, Judy."

"Two shots entered the upper torso from behind. Both exited through the chest. One most likely pierced the heart. There's a clean laceration across his throat, ear to ear. And judging by the amount of blood in the bottom of the boat, I'd say if the gunshots didn't kill him, then he certainly bled to death. I'll be able to tell you more later."

"Time of death?"

"The rigor mortis tells me it was somewhere between mid-morning and early afternoon yesterday."

"Anything else of interest?"

"It's hard to say if someone else got out of the boat here. Grass runs all the way down to the water."

"So the shooter could have been in another boat, and this one drifted up to the shore."

"Perhaps, but the bow looks like it was driven into it."

"I guess a strong current could have done it. Do lakes have currents?"

Walker shrugged. "We haven't discovered footprints anywhere in the immediate area. If someone else was in the boat, they concealed their escape route."

"A Parks employee said a road that dead ends at the edge of the park is a little north of here. A car could have been parked there."

"Yeah, I was about to mention it. One of our guys is familiar with the road."

"Let me guess. Grass on all shoulders."

"And no one living at the end of the road to notice a car."

"Thanks, Judy."

Jan turned and saw Jenny had pulled back the sheet covering Nathan Parker for a secondary examination. She walked over to where her partner was kneeling down. "Did you get a hold of Parker's office?"

"His administrative assistant lost it when I told her he was dead, but she was able to give me some information. Parker was going to meet a man named Saunders yesterday and wasn't expected to come into the office. She said he was always on the lookout for new investors and would do whatever it took to secure a deal."

"That raises a few questions."

"I thought so too. She said he didn't tell her where he was going to meet Saunders, but he would check in later in the day."

"She didn't think it was unusual when he didn't call?"

"Not until she was ready to leave the office. She called him but he didn't answer, so she left a message. She called again, left another message, and went home."

"You didn't find a phone on him when you checked earlier, right?"

"It might be in his car, wherever that is. Or it could be sitting on the bottom of the lake."

"The Parks employee said the boat belonged to a boat rental place on the other side of the lake off Seminole Boulevard. We need to talk to them."

Jenny focused on Parker's body. "Jan, look at the exit wounds in his chest. Judy said they are right at or near his heart, and about six inches apart. No doubt he was shot in the back at close range. And this throat wound is clean and precise. No jagged edges to indicate any kind of hesitation."

Jan studied the wounds. "Kind of weird, don't you think?"

"Damned efficient, I'd say."

"What I mean is, a killer usually employs one method to do the job. To use two methods seems more like--"

"Overkill?"

"Could be. Or he was sending a message. And if so, I don't like this message one bit."

Jenny offered a tight grin.. "How do you know the killer was a *he*?"

"Touché, mon amie."

Jan waited until Jenny finished with her examination, then motioned to the ambulance team. Neither detective uttered a word as they watched the paramedics hoist the body of Nathan Parker onto a stretcher and load him into the rear of the ambulance.

CHAPTER 11

Jan and Jenny drove straight to Tom and Jerry's Boat Rentals on the west side of Lake Seminole and spoke to the manager, Sylvester Katz. Upon hearing of the death of Nathan Parker, Katz was stunned "Mr. Parker is dead?" The white-haired man shook his head. "I wondered what all the sirens were about."

"Was he a regular customer of yours?" Jan said.

"Not a regular in the sense he came here every week, if that's what you mean."

"But often enough so you recognized him."

Katz nodded. "He always called ahead so I'd have a boat ready for him."

"Was anyone with him this time?"

"I didn't see them this time if there was. Mr. Parker never went fishing alone, though."

"Always someone with him, then?"

"He said the lake was a good place to talk business."

"Was it the same person each time or someone different?"

"Different people mostly, but there was one fella...oh, what was his name?" Katz laid a withered hand over his wrinkled mouth. "Wagner. Carter...no, Campbell Wagner. I remember now because I thought it was funny he had two last names when he was introduced to me. He went fishing with Mr. Parker several times."

"You were never introduced to the others with Mr. Parker?"

"Nope, he was the only one who ever came into the shop."

"Do you know anything else about Campbell Wagner?"

"Nope, just to say hello."

"Mr. Parker owns a black Mercedes S 580. One is sitting in your parking lot. Is that his?"

"I believe so. I was surprised to see it when I came in this morning."

"You didn't call him when he didn't bring your boat back yesterday?" Jenny said.

"Special privileges are given to certain customers."

"What does that mean, exactly?"

"It means that Mr. Parker is a good friend of the man who owns this shop. Besides, he never gave me his phone number."

On their way to check out Parker's car, Jenny phoned Judy Walker and requested a forensics team. "I'll bet there's not a fingerprint to be found anywhere on this car, inside or out."

"I won't take that bet," Jan said, "but if it's been wiped clean, then we'll know for certain someone did some serious planning before killing Nathan Parker."

While waiting for the forensics team, they talked to several boaters who said they often used the public boat ramp near the rental shop. Two of the regulars admitted seeing Parker on the lake but couldn't give a positive description of the person with him.

Jan and Jenny went back to the office once the forensics team arrived.

Jan stood by the clue board, reviewing the short list of evidence accumulated in their newest case. Jenny's belief Nathan Parker's car had been wiped clean proved correct. Minutes later, she shifted her attention to the scant amount of evidence on the Murphy Munyer case. No similarities between the pair existed. She shook her head at the thought of having to deal with two difficult murders.

Jenny looked up from her computer. "Jan, I'm not finding anything to indicate Nathan Parker was in any sort of financial trouble. His business affairs were never in question except one time when he was brought before the state ethics commission. Nothing was ever proven, though."

"What was that all about?"

"He was implicated in the sale of an apartment complex with substandard renovations. But the contractor wound up getting burned."

"Where was this complex located?"

"The Town 'N' Country area in Tampa."

"Tampa, huh? What was the name of the contracting company?"

"Riverview Contracting out of, where else, Riverview, Florida. They filed Chapter 13 shortly after the hearing. You think *they* may have had something to do with killing Parker?"

"Could be. They took the fall and were wiped out. Revenge is always a strong motive when there's nothing to lose." Jan noticed the time was 6:11 p.m. "Well, I'm bushed. Let's call it a day. Want to grab a beer at the Spinnaker?"

"Thanks, Jan, but I've got some shopping to do. Rick and I have a date tomorrow night."

"Going to buy a new outfit to impress your beau?"

Jenny smiled before turning to leave.

Crabby's going to be awfully disappointed when I tell him you stood him up for a younger guy, Jan thought. But having a beer and chatting with the old salt was just what she needed.

CHAPTER 12

As it turned out, Jan wound up being the one who was disappointed. When she pulled into the parking lot of the Spinnaker Bar and Grill not a single space was available. "Tourists," she muttered, feeling a strong urge to head home.

About the time she was ready to give up, two cars backed out. She thanked them under her breath as she claimed one of the spots. Her brief streak of luck ended once she walked inside. The place was brimming with people, wall-to-wall humanity. The booths were full, every bar chair taken, some of them standing beside their friends at the bar. She scanned every inch of the smoke-filled room. Adding to her discontent, Crabby was nowhere to be found. She didn't want to drink alone and turned to leave.

The scratching sound of a bar chair being dragged across the wooden floor drew her attention. A man and a woman were leaving the bar. One chair was taken immediately while the other remained empty. Jan weaved through the crowd in time to grab it and sit down. Though not situated on the end of the bar where she and Crabby preferred to roost, she rested her arms on the countertop and waited. A beer and conversation with Hank would be a pleasant end to her day.

"Afternoon, Jan," Hank said. "The usual?"

"Sure, Hank."

Jan felt uneasy sitting in the room dominated by strangers,

like she didn't belong and didn't have the right to be among them. Odd considering the number of times she'd been to the Spinnaker.

"Here you go."

"I appreciate it, Hank."

He placed a shot of whiskey and a cold mug of beer in front of her and left to attend to a man and woman sitting nearby.

Jan fingered the shot glass as her mind drifted back to the murders, but quickly turned to thoughts of Jenny and her new acquaintance. Two murders and one new chance at happiness had her considering how strange life could be. She heard the scratching of the bar chair beside her, but ignored it and threw back the shot. A healthy pull of beer helped to cool the burning liquor as it went down. As she lowered her mug, she sensed someone standing beside her.

"Excuse me, is this seat taken?" he said.

"Nope, it's all yours." She hadn't looked up before answering, and did a double take when she saw him.

His black hair was wavy and cut close to his head. A few strands of gray appeared at his temples. Six feet three inches tall or better with Mediterranean features, his steel-gray eyes were soft and in no way intimidating.

"Good," he said. "I was beginning to think I'd have to go somewhere else." His demeanor was relaxed and natural.

Jan lowered her eyes back to her beer. An emotion she'd long since dismissed began to stir her insides.

"What'll it be?" Hank said to the man.

"Winding Creek on the rocks. And bring the lady whatever she's having."

"Just a beer, Hank," Jan said. She smiled at the handsome new arrival. This was the second time in less than a year someone had addressed her as a lady, Crabby being the first at the beginning of their friendship.

"Comin' right up," Hank said.

The stranger looked around the room. "Boy, this place is

really crowded."

"Tourists. Normally it's not like this."

The stranger grinned. "I guess that includes me. I just stopped in to relax after a long day."

"So, where are you from?"

"Fort Lee, New Jersey. I'm down here for a couple of weeks on business."

"What sort of business?"

"I'm a software salesman. I'm interviewing prospective clients in Tampa."

"What brings you to this side of the bay?"

"The beaches, of course. Tampa's too big a city for my taste. One of my associates suggested I stay on the beaches."

"Well, you picked a good spot. Treasure Island is one of the finest communities around."

Hank returned with their drinks and arched an eyebrow at Jan before leaving.

"By the way, my name is Max Castle. And you are?"

"Jan Larkin. Pleased to make your acquaintance, Max."

Castle picked up his glass and held it out. Jan mirrored the gesture with her mug. They clinked their drinks together.

"So what do you do, Jan?"

"I work for the county sheriff's office."

Castle sipped his whiskey. "A detective, huh?"

Jan was surprised, but held it inside. "How could you possibly know that?"

"Just a lucky guess. I was going to say administrative assistant, but I was afraid I might insult you. Are you working on any interesting cases, Jan?"

Her eyes left his for the counter.

"Uh-oh. I guess that was the wrong thing to say. Sorry if I was out of line."

"No, Max, it's okay. I'm in Homicide, and right now we've got a couple of really tough cases."

"Homicide, huh? Boy, I don't think I could handle being in

that line of work.

Seeing all those, uh…well, you know what I mean."

Jan took a drink of beer. "Yes, I do. I've been handling it for quite a long time."

"If you don't mind me asking, how long is a long time?"

"Twelve years. Some days it seems like my whole life."

Castle took another sip of whiskey.

Moments without conversation filled with the chatter and boisterous laughter from those around them.

"Well, I probably should be getting home," Jan said.

"So soon?"

"My day is catching up to me."

"Excuse me for being so bold, but would you care to join me for dinner? I really hate eating alone, and I'd love to continue our conversation."

Jan was close to accepting the stranger's invitation, but the voice of caution advised her to beg off. "Maybe some other time, Max. I'm really tired."

"Well, the offer stands. Do you come here often?"

"As often as I can."

Castle raised his glass. "Until next time then."

His smile was as alluring as his looks, but Jan found the strength not to gaze over her shoulder before she waved to Hank and walked out the door.

CHAPTER 13

In their attempt to dig further into the murders of Murphy Munyer and Nathan Parker, Jan and Jenny hit dead end after dead end over the next two days. Jenny was glued to her computer in an effort to uncover more information about the victims when Jan approached her.

"Jenny, I forgot to ask you about your date with...Rick? Is that his name?"

Her partner's smiling face appeared from the side of the monitor. Her eyes were glimmering. "It was wonderful. Simply wonderful. We went to Madeira Beach and had dinner at Devin's Seafood Saloon. Then he surprised me with a bottle of wine. We took a blanket out on the beach and talked for hours. Did I mention it was simply wonderful?"

Jan remembered the happiness she felt when she was first dating Ken, her ex-husband, and part of her celebrated Jenny's newfound happiness. But a part of her worried her friend was moving too fast, seeing only what she wanted to see, and not what was really there. "What does he do?"

Jenny's smile lessened. "He's unemployed right now. He just moved here and is living in a house in Seminole his family owns. But he's a salesman, and he's certain he can find a job real soon. He has such a positive and upbeat attitude about everything. I know it's just a matter of time."

The memory of her former partner, Seeward Sinclair, slipped

into Jan's mind. He used to live in Seminole. "Jenny, that's great. I've been meaning to tell you about—"

The telephone rang and interrupted her. Jenny scooped up the receiver. "All right. Send him in." She wore a puzzled expression as she hung up the phone. "Jan, a Dr. Roland Charles is here to see you."

"Good! He's the guy from the university I told you about. The encryption expert. Maybe he's got some answers about the Munyer disc."

Charles strode into the office and greeted Jan without hesitation. "Jan, it's so good to see you again. It's been such a long time." His tenor voice rang sincere as he kissed her cheek and hugged her.

An inch under six feet tall, his receding silver hair was pulled into a small ponytail, accenting the sharp features of his face. His gray, waist-length jacket hung snug over a collared navy blue polo shirt that didn't hide a slight paunch. His sharply creased jeans ended at the top of his brown deck shoes, completing the attire of the college professor.

Jan accepted his friendly gesture. "Good to see *you* again, Roland." She glanced at Jenny and saw her partner wearing an impish grin. "And this is Detective Jenny Lester."

Charles turned and smiled as he nodded. "A pleasure to meet you, Detective Lester. Jan...uh, Sergeant Larkin and I go way back."

Jenny nodded and her smile grew wider.

"Were you able to make anything of the disc I sent you, Roland?" Jan asked.

"Yes, yes, I have the information right here. Do you mind if I sit down?" He pulled a folded piece of paper and the disc from the pocket of his jacket and took a seat at her desk. "To begin with, the numbers are letters and the letters are numbers. I started with zero followed by 1 through 9 in a row. Then I wrote the letters of the alphabet underneath them, A under zero, B under one, C under two, and so forth."

Jan peered over his shoulder.

Jenny pushed her chair over close to him, sat down, and copied his instructions in her notepad. "So, let me see if I understand you. My name. Jenny, would be…94334 in this code. Is that right?"

Charles grinned. "Yes, as I have it written. But whoever devised the code on the CD subtracted three numbers from that of the corresponding letter."

"Okay." She mouthed his instructions. "So my name would be…61001."

"Correct."

"Is the same combination used for the group of numbers, Roland?" Jan asked.

"No. For the numbers, two letters were added. Thus, two hundred fifty would read EHC. Where it got a little tricky was in the numbers to letters combination of each of the five rows. For example, you see the letters FGHEIHKEE at the end of the first row.

Those letters translate to 34265822 using the letters A through J on my list. RTQVPRQNM at the end of the second row translate to 574935410 using the letters K through T on my list. In other words, the first row of letters from the disc starts with the first row of letters on my list. The second row of letters from the disc starts with the second row of letters from my list." Charles looked up at her. "Do you follow?"

"I think I've got it," Jenny said as she scribbled down the information.

"I'm glad one of us does," Jan said.

Charles laughed. "Suffice to say, the five rows of numbers and letters from the disc are the names of five people, the names of banks, and an amount of money that, I assume, is in each person's account in those banks." He covered the answers to all the letters and numbers he'd written down on the paper then showed Jenny a coded line. "See if you can decipher this."

When she had written it down, he showed the line to Jan and

handed her the paper. They didn't wait long.

"Okay, here goes," Jenny said. "Murphy Munyer, Royal Bank of Grand Cayman, three million, four hundred fifty-two thousand, six hundred fifty-eight dollars and ten cents."

"You got it, partner. Down to the penny. Nathan Parker has an account there, too.

A Campbell Wagner and a Leonard Hobson have accounts at the Islands Savings and Trust, and an Avery Clendenon at the Grand Island Reserve. Some have more money than Munyer and some less." Jan studied the list of names. "They must be involved in some sort of partnership. But what *sort* of partnership is the question."

"I hope this helps you, Jan," Charles said. "And I feel I must tell you in the world of coded messages, this one was pretty simple to break."

"It will definitely help us. Thank you, Roland."

"Well, I must be getting back to the university. I have a class in an hour." Charles turned to Jenny. "It was a pleasure to meet you, Detective Lester." As he rose and started for the door, he turned to Jan. "Stay in touch."

Jenny waited until he was gone. "Jan, we know two of these guys are dead. This might also be some sort of a hit list."

"It's entirely possible. But if that's the case, doesn't it seem odd to you Munyer would have the list?"

"I see what you mean." Jenny paused, thinking. "What if they all had a copy of the list?"

"What would be the point of having a copy? The list is in code."

"True. But, for whatever reason, suppose they did, and one of the partners deciphered the code. He may have gotten greedy after seeing the numbers."

"Or someone outside of the partnership may have stolen the list and is trying to get them to help him break the code before he kills them."

Focused on the theories they were tossing around, neither

Jan nor Jenny heard Detective Sam Vanderschied walk up behind them.

"Jan, I couldn't help but overhear you," he said. "Campbell Wagner was found dead in the parking lot of Angora's Lounge two nights ago. I heard it on the news."

"And Sylvester Katz, the manager of the boat rental business on Lake Seminole, said he often went fishing with Nathan Parker."

"Damn it, that's right!" Jenny said. "I knew that name sounded familiar. His administrative assistant said he was out of the office when I called. She never called me back."

"Thanks, Sam," Jan said.

"Glad I could help." Vanderschied turned and left them for his desk.

"Jan, there's something else about this list that has me curious," Jenny said. The impish grin returned to her face.

The senior detective picked up the paper and studied it. "What about it?"

"Just how far back *do* you and the professor go?"

"What?"

"Well, I mean, he walks in and gives you a big hug and a kiss. You know, one might think you and he are closer than you want people to believe."

Jan sighed. "Five years ago, my ex-husband and I met Roland at a party. When I told him I was a detective, he offered his services."

"Offered his services?" Jenny's grin widened.

"His area of expertise, Detective Nosey, and nothing else."

"Oh, I don't know. He seemed awful friendly for someone who just wants to help."

Jan rolled her eyes. "He was married at the time. The four of us met for dinner on several occasions and..." She stopped when Jenny began to laugh. "Detective, before you become a bigger pain in the ass than you already are, would you call Indian Rocks Beach P.D. and find out what they know about Campbell Wagner?"

Jenny was still laughing when she picked up the receiver.

Jan left her desk for the clue board to add the information provided by Roland Charles. As she noted the new findings, she theorized. Someone had eliminated three wealthy men with hefty offshore bank accounts. A similar fate might await Leonard Hobson and Avery Clendenon. Besides gaining access to their secret fortune, was there a lesser known motive for these men being eliminated? And by whom?

Jenny ended her phone call and joined her partner at the clue board. "Okay,

Campbell Wagner was poisoned by a puncture wound to the palm of his right hand.

Death was almost instantaneous, according to the preliminary report."

"Poisoned? In a parking lot?"

"He was still inside his car. They're not exactly sure what kind of poison killed him."

"Sort of makes me wonder how someone could get a hold of something that lethal."

"Wagner is president of the Gulf Savings and Trust Bank. He's married and has no children. No one at the scene saw anything unusual or noticed anyone having a conversation with him. Does this sound familiar?"

"Yeah. Like our other cases. Find out all you can about Hobson and Clendenon. Then call them to set up interviews."

Jenny returned to her desk and ran a quick search on Hobson and Clendenon, then made a few phone calls.

Jan was still standing in front of the clue board when Jenny approached her.

"Well, like the others on the list, Hobson and Clendenon have different occupations," Jenny said. "Hobson owns and operates Hobson's New and Used Yacht Sales at Maximo Moorings in south St. Petersburg. Clendenon owns five restaurants throughout Hillsborough County. Three of the restaurants boast five-star ratings."

"They're all definitely part of a high rollers club."

"I talked to Avery Clendenon, and the soonest he can see us is tomorrow.

"Tomorrow? I want to talk to him now."

"I told him today would be better, but he wasn't having any of it. He tried to sound nonchalant, but I could tell he was very uncomfortable. I called Leonard Hobson, but his administrative assistant said he was tending to a family emergency. I told her it was important he call me back."

"Those two have to know about the others. Why are they blowing us off?"

"I also called a friend of mine at Tampa P.D. about Clendenon. You know, to see if they had anything on him."

"Did they give you any useful information?"

Jenny hesitated and swallowed. "He has no criminal record, but it seems one of his restaurants, Osvaldo's, is a favorite haunt of Colby Rittenhouse."

"Colby Rittenhouse!"

A rush of anger reddened Jan's face. The exonerated crime boss had ordered the murder of District Attorney David Ballentine's daughter Janie. His bodyguard, Eddie Papalos, had been responsible for killing Janie Ballantine and Jan's former partner, Seeward Sinclair. She had never forgiven herself for not knowing Seeward was going to confront Papalos at the farmhouse in Brandon.

"He likes to hold meetings in one of the private rooms there."

Jan's silence was deafening as her hate for Rittenhouse smoldered. "I think we should call it a day, Jenny. I'm losing my train of thought."

"What say we hit the Spinnaker for a beer or ten?"

"Good idea, partner." Jan huffed between breaths.

Jenny went to her desk to call Hank the bartender. "Jan, the Spinnaker is packed, but Hank says Crabby already grabbed a booth. He was hoping we'd drop by. But he also said something's bothering Crabby."

"What do you mean?"

"Crabby just keeps staring at his beer and mumbling. I told Hank we'd be there soon."

As Jan's intense aversion to Colby Rittenhouse lingered, she wondered what could possibly annoy Crabby.

CHAPTER 14

When Jan and Jenny arrived at the Spinnaker, Jan slid in beside Crabby while Jenny sat down across from them. Neither acknowledged their friend, and both wore a look of disappointment. Crabby nodded to Jenny, who motioned at Jan with her head.

"I'll get us a couple of beers, Jan," she said.

"No, I'll get them." Jan swung her legs from under the table and lifted herself out of the booth. She took her time getting to the bar, still annoyed by the information connecting Avery Clendenon and Colby Rittenhouse Jenny had uncovered.

Hank was waiting for her. "Hi, Jan, you having the usual?"

"Hey, Hank." She offered a weak smile. "I guess we're getting predictable." She lowered her eyes to the counter as he went to get their drinks.

"Hello, Jan," a man said.

Jan recognized his voice before she looked up. "Max! What are you doing here?"

He grinned. "Looking for you."

She laughed. "I was wondering how long you'd be here."

"A few more days."

Hank returned with a tray of drinks and set them on the counter. "Here you go, Jan." He cut a glance at Castle. "Give me a minute and I'll be right over."

"I'll take care of it, Hank," Castle said and set his glass of

Winding Creek whiskey on the tray.

"Why, thank you, Max," Jan said.

"Yeah, thanks," Hank said.

"Oh, Hank, I need a shot for Jenny."

"Really? That's a first. I'll be right back."

"Have you thought more about my offer for dinner?" Castle said.

"Honestly, no, Max. I've been so busy I haven't had time to—"

"Here's your shot, Jan," Hank said.

"Thanks, Hank."

"Yeah." Hank cut a glance at Castle again and left.

Castle picked up the tray. "Shall we?"

When they reached the booth, he set the tray on the table,

"Jenny, Crabby, I'd like you to meet Max Castle," Jan said.

"The pleasure is all mine," Castle said. He nodded to Crabby, then settled his gray eyes on Jenny. "Jan, you neglected to tell me your partner was so attractive."

Jenny smiled, rose, and moved into the booth beside Crabby.

"Of course I didn't," Jan said. "I don't need the competition."

She and her new acquaintance sat down, and she distributed the shots of bourbon and beers.

Castle picked up his glass of whiskey and looked at Crabby. "Sir, I can't help but wonder how you acquired the nickname Crabby."

Jan and Jenny burst into laughter.

"Uh-oh. Did I say something wrong?"

Crabby scowled. "Naw, it ain't that."

"He gets a little cranky at times," Jenny said.

"An' these two never lets me fergit it neither."

"Okay, everybody, time for a toast," Jan said.

Castle raised his glass and Crabby, his shot, but Jenny didn't move. She stared at the splash of liquor sitting in front of her with uneasy eyes.

"Come on, Jenny, pick up your glass."

"I don't know, Jan. What is this stuff?"

"Kentucky straight."

"I don't do shots often, and it's usually rum."

"Aw, don't be a baby. This is a special toast."

Jenny smiled at Castle and picked up the glass.

"Here's to good friends and new friends," Jan said, and threw back the bourbon.

Crabby matched her, as did Castle, but Jenny continued to ponder the shot glass. With the others watching, she took a slow, deep breath and tossed it down. A second later, her blue eyes went wide as saucers, and she started to cough. "That wasn't so bad," she whispered.

The others howled with laughter at the sight of her first bout with the bourbon.

"Well, it's certainly been a pleasure meeting all of you, but I have to run," Castle said.

"Not now, Max," Jan said. "We're just getting started."

"I know, and I wish I could stay, but I have a business dinner to attend. Duty calls."

Jan leaned into him. "Then let me walk you out."

Castle bid Jenny and Crabby farewell, then he and Jan slowly made their way through the tables and cigarette smoke to the front door. "Jan, I hope you can find time to have dinner with me before I leave."

"I'll do my best, Max."

"Your two friends seem like very nice people."

"They're the best, as far as I'm concerned."

He gazed into her eyes. "You have a good evening, Jan." He smiled, then turned and walked out the door.

Jan sighed as a sensation she'd known years ago rose up inside her. Being desired by a man as handsome as Max was a wonderful feeling. Her skin tingled as she made her way back to Jenny and Crabby. As she neared the booth, Jenny was poking Crabby in the ribs and laughing.

Crabby slapped her hand away. "Now stop that!"

"What's going on here?" Jan said.

"Oh, nothing," Jenny said. "Crabby and I were just having a friendly debate."

"Are you sure that's all you were doing?"

Crabby smiled, revealing his yellow-stained teeth.

Jan eyed both of her friends suspiciously before she sat down. Then she leaned forward. "Guess who has a date tomorrow night?"

CHAPTER 15

Jan stood in the parking lot of the Spinnaker Bar and Grill and looked up at the clear night sky. "Don't the stars look beautiful tonight? And there are so many of them."

"Are you sure it's not the stars in your eyes?" Jenny said.

Jan twisted her mouth in disgust. "All right, so I'm thinking about Max. But you have to admit, he *is* very handsome."

"He reminds me of George, uh... Oh, you know who I mean, Jan."

"George Clooney?" Jan sighed. "I thought the same thing when I first met him."

Jenny was about to tease her some more, but her phone rang before she had the chance. Her blue eyes brightened when she saw the name on the screen. "Ricky," she mouthed to Jan. "Well, how did it go? Ricky, that's great! Let's hope the next one seals the deal."

Jan covered her mouth so she wouldn't be heard laughing and turned away. It was the first time she'd heard her partner refer to her new friend as Ricky.

"Oh, Ricky, I don't know. I've been at the Spinnaker with Jan and Crabby. I don't know if I that's a good idea." Jenny lowered her phone. "Jan, he wants to see me right now."

"Then what are you waiting for?"

"Ricky, where do you want me to meet you? Okay. See you in thirty minutes." She shoved the phone into her pants pocket.

"He's excited about an interview he had today. The owner asked him to come back tomorrow for a second interview. He wants to tell me all about it."

Jan wore a wry smile as she nodded.

"All right, what's with the look?"

"I'm just so happy for...*Ricky*."

"So, I call him Ricky. So what?"

"Oh, nothing. Ricky Lennon just sounds so cute. Does *Ricky* think he'll get the job?"

"Enough already!" Jenny started to laugh. "I have to go."

"By all means, and tell *Ricky* I said hello."

Jan couldn't stop laughing as she watched Jenny climb into her car.

CHAPTER 16

Jan was still laughing about the mischievous tormenting she'd dealt her love-struck partner when she pulled up to her house in Largo. She felt good for a change, and the reason was clear. Max Castle. Feeling good about someone had been a long time in coming.

As she closed the car door, she thought of him and the chemistry developing between them, though she knew it was much too soon to be sure. Still, excitement was building inside her at the prospect of their next meeting. She was about to open the front door when the phone distracted her.

"Now who the hell is calling me at this hour?"

No name or number appeared on the caller ID.

"Jan, Stan Jeffries here. Sorry to call you so late."

"Stan! Oh, my god! What a pleasant surprise."

She and Jeffries had been involved in a brief relationship shortly after her divorce from Ken. He was interested in a permanent arrangement. She was looking for someone to lean on. They stopped dating after a time but had remained good friends.

"I can't remember the last time we spoke," she said. "How *are* you?"

"I've been better. I'm down here at Maximo Moorings investigating the murder of a Leonard Hobson. If you have the time, I'd like to pick your brain."

The mention of Hobson's name chased a shiver down her spine. "Well sure, Stan. How can I help you?"

"I found the phone number of a Nathan Parker on Hobson's cell phone contact list. Aren't you handling that case?"

"You always did have a good memory. He was a developer. A little light in the ethics department we've been told. We're not having much luck with the case."

"That's too bad. I was hoping there might be a connection between him and Hobson. We haven't been able to uncover any evidence at the scene."

"Stan, there are a few things you should know. I was just about to go into my house. Give me a minute." She opened the door, turned on the overhead light, and flopped down on the sofa.

She went on to explain about their investigation of Murphy Munyer, their discovery of the coded information disc in his condo, and their suspicion Munyer, Parker, Hobson, Campbell Wagner, and Avery Clendenon were all involved in some sort of silent partnership.

"Jan, Wagner was also on Hobson's list of contacts. Do you think there's a particular reason they're being killed off?"

"My partner and I were wondering the same thing, Stan, but we don't know what that reason might be."

"I spoke with Miriam Harvey, Hobson's administrative assistant. I asked her if she had ever met Nathan Parker. She said she hadn't."

"I'm beginning to wonder if all of them were the money merchants while someone else was calling the shots."

"A possibility. I asked Harvey if Hobson had many appointments today, and she said he only had one at nine-thirty this morning. But another man showed up unannounced later in the day."

"Interesting. She told my partner he was busy with a family emergency. Who did Hobson meet with at nine-thirty?"

"A fellow named Richard Lennon."

Jan cringed. She hoped it was a coincidence Jenny's new acquaintance had the same name. "Was this Richard Lennon interested in buying a boat?"

"It was a job interview. Harvey said Hobson was looking to hire a new salesperson."

"And this other man showed up without an appointment?"

"According to Harvey it wasn't unusual, but it didn't happen very often. She said his name was Townsend, that Hobson was reluctant to see him at first. Once they spoke in private, Hobson seemed okay. She said Hobson always took on a certain expression when he was about to make a big sale. Hobson told her Townsend wanted to look at some of the yachts, and they would return when they were done. That was the last she saw of either of them."

"Did this man give her any other name than Townsend?"

"Townsend was all he said."

"Did anyone else see this man?"

"Townsend arrived just as they were about to close. The other workers had all gone home. All except for James Monroe, the dockmaster."

"Where was Monroe at the time?"

"Harvey wasn't exactly sure. He said he had to check on another boat on the far side of the marina before he left. We went to his apartment, but he wasn't home."

"Was it standard procedure for Monroe to leave work without checking in first?"

"Harvey didn't say."

"Did you get a description of Townsend?"

"Harvey said he was tall, had red hair, brown eyes, and was very well dressed, but a little overweight. I'll send you a better description and some other info tomorrow."

"Thanks, Stan. I'll send you everything we have on our cases. You never know if they might be connected."

"Jan, you've been a big help. Let's keep in touch as much as possible, okay?"

"Good idea and good luck."

"On a personal note, if you ever change your mind...about us, I mean, don't hesitate to call me."

"I will, and goodnight, Stan."

Jan got to her feet and turned off the light. Sleep would be slow in finding her tonight.

CHAPTER 17

Jan was already in the office when Jenny arrived the next morning. Standing like a statue in front of the clue board, her left arm lay across her stomach in support of her right, her hand gently pulling on her chin. Jan's fascination with the information written on the board lured Jenny to her side.

"Oh, no!" Jenny said. "Now Hobson's dead?"

"Stan Jeffries, an acquaintance and homicide detective with St. Pete P.D., called me last night. He emailed the pictures and information this morning. Hobson's personal secretary told Jeffries Hobson had an appointment yesterday morning and an unscheduled appointment later in the day. She gave them a basic description of a man they now believe to be the suspect, but no one saw the guy leave after he met with Hobson. And, of course, there was no evidence found at the crime scene."

Jenny leaned forward. "Is that an ice pick sticking out of the back of Hobson's head?"

"By the depth of penetration, I'd say the guy who killed him was strong."

"That just leaves Avery Clendenon. Let's hope he doesn't get it before we talk to him."

"What time are we supposed to meet with him?"

"Ten-thirty at, uh...Osvaldo's." Jenny looked at her watch. "Maybe we should leave now and go by his house first."

Jan didn't answer, suddenly tasting the bitter bile in her

throat. The restaurant would always be associated with Colby Rittenhouse.

Jenny turned to go back to her desk.

"How did it go with Rick last night?"

"Fine. We had a good time."

"And he was excited about his interview yesterday morning?"

"He, uh, said it went well."

"And did he mention his interview was with Leonard Hobson?"

"I was going to tell you, Jan. Honest. But just now, when I saw one of the composite drawings from St. Pete P. D. on the board, I didn't want to…"

"You didn't want to believe it might be him?"

The young detective hung her head.

"Let's have a seat. I want to run something by you." Jan leaned back and narrowed her eyes. "We're trying to figure out who did what with whom concerning these five men. Let's go over what we have so far."

Jenny nodded and focused on her partner.

"We found the names of these guys on a disc in Murphy Munyer's condo. But we found nothing to indicate he knew of or ever met any of them. We know Nathan Parker and Campbell Wagner knew one another. Sylvester Katz swore to it in his statement and so did Parker's administrative assistant. She also said Parker spoke to Avery Clendenon from time to time. And Wagner's administrative assistant told Indian Rocks Beach police *he* knew Clendenon." Jan paused.

"I'm right there with you, Jan."

"I talked with Stan Jeffries again this morning. He verified Leonard Hobson *also* knew Wagner. They probably collaborated for bank transactions in regard to boat sales. So, we know for certain Parker, Wagner, and Hobson dealt with one another in some way, and they all knew Avery Clendenon. But what we don't know is whether one or all of them ever dealt with

Murphy Munyer."

"Maybe Munyer didn't associate with any of them. I mean, maybe he just invested money into whatever deal was going down."

"True, and for that matter, they all may have been silent partners. But someone had to initiate the transactions. Someone had to contact them when a new deal came up."

"Maybe someone outside of this group was calling the shots. You know, for a percentage. There's something else that's been bothering me. We know Munyer, Parker, Wagner, and Hobson were killed in different ways. Why run the risk of attracting attention by using different methods? Why not just shoot them and get it over quickly? The killer is lucky no one has gotten a good look at him."

"Maybe he enjoys the thrill of the kill." Jan stared at her partner for several seconds. "You've never told me what your boyfriend looks like."

"Well, he's six one or six two. Blonde hair, blue eyes, and he's in good shape. And he's strong."

"How do you know he's strong?"

"Last night, he was excited about how well his interview went, and he picked me up and whirled me around. Right before he kissed me."

Jan produced a tight smile. "You can relax, Jenny. He was the nine-thirty appointment, but he doesn't fit the description of the man last seen with Hobson."

"Whew! That's good to know. But, Jan, we haven't found one similarity in any of these murders. And I still don't understand why this guy killed them in so many different ways."

"Is that what's really bothering you, partner?"

"For one thing, this guy appears to be extremely efficient in dealing death. He might be a trained killer. You know, like someone who's been instructed in how to utilize various methods of getting the job done."

"I hope you're wrong, because the last thing we need is to be looking for a professional assassin."

They both understood a trained killer seldom made mistakes. And worse, when his assignment was completed, he would disappear and never be heard from again. For the next hour, they tossed around several theories before leaving for their appointment with Avery Clendenon.

CHAPTER 18

At ten thirty, Jan and Jenny approached the solid oak doors of Osvaldo's Ristorante in Tampa. Stepping inside the establishment was like taking a journey back in time. Hibiscus carpeting covered every square inch of the floor. Each table and high-backed chair in the dining area was made from black oak. Red velour rose up the walls until meeting the chandelier-filled ceilings overhead. One could only imagine what elegance graced the rooms labeled *By Special Reservation Only*.

"I'll bet the menus are embossed in gold and don't have the prices listed," Jenny whispered.

"Why are you whispering?" Jan asked.

"Because I don't feel like we belong here."

"Our badges say we do."

The maître d soon greeted them', a distinguished-looking gentleman in his forties wearing a black tailor-made tuxedo.

"My apologies, ladies," he said, "but service does not begin until eleven-thirty." He looked them up and down. "However, if you would care to enjoy a cocktail while you wait."

"We're here to see Avery Clendenon," Jan said and held up her badge.

"I see. And Mr. Clendenon is expecting you?"

"No need to trouble yourself. Is his office in the back? We can find the way."

The staunch gentleman eyed them coldly. "If you would

accompany me, please." He led them to a door in the rear marked Private, knocked twice, and opened it, gesturing Jan and Jenny inside. "Ms. Shepherd, these ladies wish to see Mr. Clendenon."

A woman in her late twenties wearing wire-rimmed glasses looked up from the laptop sitting on top of her mahogany desk. Her blonde hair was pulled into a low bun, and her cobalt eyes were a cool contrast to her black business suit.

Giving Jan and Jenny the once-over, she rose and went to a door several feet from her desk, knocked twice, and eased it open. "Mr. Clendenon, your ten-thirty appointment has arrived." She pulled the door open wider and turned to the detectives. "Mr. Clendenon will see you now."

Avery Clendenon stood in the middle of his large office sporting a smile that was as greasy as the slicked-back black fringe encircling his bald head. He was short and as big around as he was tall, with a smattering of hair across his upper lip. His ill-fitting blue suit gave him the appearance of a third-rate pimp.

"Please come in, detectives," he said. "I've been expecting you."

Jan stepped forward. "I'm Detective Sergeant Larkin and this is Detective Lester, Pinellas County Sheriff's Office."

"Won't you sit down?" Clendenon kept his smile as he rounded his monstrous desk and settled into a high-backed leather chair. "Now, how may I assist you?"

The detectives remained standing.

"Do you know a man named Murphy Munyer?" Jan said.

"No, I don't believe I do."

"Have any of your associates ever mentioned his name?"

"I've never heard them speak of anyone... Wait! What, exactly, do you mean by *my associates*?"

"Your business partners, Nathan Parker and Campbell Wagner."

Clendenon's smile vanished under the threads of his moustache. "That was terrible what happened to them. Just terrible.

I'm still in shock."

"But you've never heard them mention his name?"

Clendenon dropped his head, thinking. "No, I can't say that I have."

"Do you know Leonard Hobson?"

Clendenon jerked his head up. "Why, yes. Yes, I do. He's been in here a few times. On occasion, I've sent some people to see him. You know, concerning business."

"What sort of business?"

"They were looking to buy boats."

"Are you aware he was murdered yesterday?"

"I found out this morning. Terrible. Just terrible."

"We understand you, Mr. Parker, and Mr. Wagner were partners. In what sort of business dealings were you involved, Mr. Clendenon?"

"I don't believe that's any of your concern, Detective."

"Mr. Clendenon, three of your associates are dead. Another man, whom you say you don't know but is somehow connected to all of you, is also dead. Why won't you tell me what sort of business dealings in which you and the others were involved?"

Clendenon shifted in his chair, then leaned back and folded his hands over his protruding stomach. "I don't wish to answer any more of your questions, Detective. And in the future, I suggest you contact my attorney."

Neither Jan nor Jenny moved.

"You don't wish to help us find the killer of your associates?" Jan said.

Clendenon's answer was another greasy smile.

"Thank you for your time, sir. And good luck."

The pair left Clendenon's office and walked into the main dining area.

"Is that guy hiding something or what?" Jenny said.

Jan looked straight ahead as the snobbish maître d' eyed them on their way out. A few steps from the entrance, the richly carved doors parted, and a man surrounded by four other men entered. The group came to a halt in front of the women.

The man in the middle was trim and well over six feet tall, his thick brown hair overrun by channels of silver. His sharp blue eyes settled on Jan and Jenny. "Boys, where are your manners? Let these ladies through." He stepped back and gestured with his arm.

Anger spread like wildfire through Jan, and she glared at Colby Rittenhouse as she and Jenny passed by.

"Nice ass," he said.

Jan spun around and started to charge him.

Jenny grabbed hold of her arm. "Easy, Sergeant. He's not worth it."

A chorus of callous laughter sounded behind them as they left the restaurant. Well into the pack of cars filling the parking lot, Jenny let go of Jan's arm.

"You looked like you wanted to kill him, Jan."

"I do want to kill him."

Jenny didn't answer, waiting until they got into their car. "Since we're in Tampa, why don't we check out Clendenon's other restaurants and see if anyone will talk."

Jan took a deep breath. "Now that's a good idea, partner."

The trip to the other restaurants proved to be a waste of time, and frustration stayed with the detectives on their drive back to their office in Largo.

Jan retired to her usual position in front of the clue board and began to reassess the information.

Jenny fell into the chair at her desk and stared blankly at her computer monitor.

Remembering something too important to ignore, she wheeled her chair around. "Jan, it's almost four o'clock."

"So?"

"Have you forgotten you have a date with Max Castle tonight?"

"Aw, damn it!" Jan spun on her heels and hurried to her desk. "Can you make sure —"

"Go on, get out of here. I'll finish up."
Jenny laughed as she watched her partner dash out the door.

CHAPTER 19

Jan put on some speed in her attempt to race home, but the red lights at every intersection worked against her. The time she spent waiting allowed for too many thoughts. One thought above all the others made her increasingly annoyed. This was her first date in years, and she realized she had nothing to wear. New additions to her wardrobe was not something she'd considered lately. And why had she agreed to go out with Max Castle? He would be going back to New Jersey soon.

When she finally got home, she went straight to her bedroom and looked over the scant wardrobe selection lining her closet. "I don't believe it." she groused as she stripped off her clothes. "Everything I own makes me look like a cop." Sorting through her unenviable collection of pantsuits, the burgundy three-quarter sleeve dress she wore to weddings and funerals looked appealing. "You'll have to do, old girl." She laughed. "Like I have a choice." She plucked it from the clothes rack and tossed it on her bed.

A quick shower followed by a limited application of make-up created a woman hidden from the public eye for a number of years. Standing in front of the undersized mirror above the bathroom sink, Jan was surprised by the face that stared back. Though not arranged in a fashionable coif, her caramel-brown hair neatly surrounded her face. And her tired brown eyes were sparkling. "If Crabby could see me now, he wouldn't believe it." Grinning, she stepped back and examined herself. "Not too bad."

On the way to the bedroom, her phone put the brakes on her attempt to continue dressing. She groaned in anticipation of hearing more bad news from the office.

"Jan, it's Max. Are we still on for tonight?"

His voice sent a wave of excitement through her body. "Of course. Why do you ask?"

"Because I know you've been working hard lately, and I understand the unexpected demands of your job. I was just double-checking in case something had come up."

"No, we're good. I'm just getting ready and sorting through my wardrobe."

"I made a reservation for us at a place called The Garden Trellis on Clearwater Beach. I'm told it's nice. I hope it meets with your approval."

Jan's heart sank. The Garden Trellis was an elegant restaurant, and not unlike the five-star rated Osvaldo's in Tampa. "Well, Max, I'm sure it will, but, uh…"

"Is something the matter, Jan? You sound uneasy."

She sighed. "Max, I'm flattered you would take me to such a fine restaurant,

but I would really feel out of place going there. I hope you understand."

"No problem. I'll call and cancel our reservation. Is there somewhere you'd prefer to go?"

Jan filed through the list of places that quickly came to mind, eliminating those that might cause him to think less of her. "Ralston's Seafood House in St. Pete Beach is good. Do you like seafood?"

"Can't get enough of it. I'll come by for you in half an hour."

Caution iced Jan's insides. She didn't want him to know where she lived. Not yet anyway. "Max, to be perfectly honest, I'm running late. How about I meet you there? Say in an hour?"

"No problem. Just give me the directions."

She gave him the address to the eatery on Corey Avenue and suggested the best route for him to follow.

After the call ended, Jan examined her choice of apparel again.

Sorting through my wardrobe. What a stupid thing to say.

She slipped on the burgundy dress, along with a pair of black patent leather heels, and checked out the woman appearing in the rectangular mirror hanging on her bedroom wall. She struck a pose, then turned to the left and right in an effort to gain approval from her toughest critic.

"Damn, girl! Where have you been hiding?"

CHAPTER 20

Jan felt the same sense of dread she experienced when performing certain aspects of her job. But the feeling that weighed on her as she approached Ralston's Seafood House was unusual in a way. And she knew why. Agreeing to have dinner with Max was a huge mistake. She wasn't ready to play this game and considered leaving. Figured she'd lie to him about getting a call from work. She hesitated mere steps away from the entrance. Lying wasn't a part of her character. And she despised anyone who lied to her. As had happened with the feeling of dread, there came a strong sense of pride that chased her uneasiness away. She deserved to be treated like a lady by a handsome man. And this man gave every indication of being respectable. He would be gone in a week, anyway. She threw back her head, opened the door, and sauntered into the restaurant.

The drone of conversation from the crowd of patrons filled her ears. In no hurry, she scanned the room. Unable to spot him, she entertained the notion maybe he'd gotten lost or had changed his mind. She walked into the modest lounge to the right of the entrance feeling a tinge of rejection and looked over a number of people waiting to be paged. She spied him at the bar, sipping his favorite drink, no doubt. She was taken by the fact even while sitting down, he stood apart from the others—like someone of importance in a sea of commoners.

Strolling toward him, she held her breath and hoped her high heels wouldn't cause her to misstep and stumble. When she got to his chair, she pushed in beside him and waited to be noticed.

Castle seemed disinterested as he turned and glanced at her. He looked away and sipped his drink a second later.

"Max?" she said.

He looked at her again. "I beg your pardon. Do I know you?"

She grinned and slapped him on the shoulder. "Will you knock it off?"

His laughter was brimming with warmth. "Sorry, but I couldn't resist. I must admit you do look entirely different than Jan the cop."

"You like?"

His eyes trailed over her.. "Oh, I *definitely* like."

He started to offer his chair when the lights on the pager in front of the man seated next to Jan glittered. The man smiled at her, stood up, and pulled out the chair.

Jan thanked the man and caught the bartender's eye. "I'll have what he's having."

"One Winding Creek on the rocks, comin' right up," the redhead said.

"There's a twenty-minute wait," Castle said.

"Good. That will give us some time to talk. So, how was your day?"

Castle continued to smile, but his steel-gray eyes told a different story. "It didn't go as well as I'd liked. To tell you the truth, I'm not having much luck down here."

The bartender returned, placed the bourbon in front of Jan, and looked at Castle. He nodded.

Jan picked up her drink and took a sip. "Well, there's always tomorrow."

"There's always tomorrow," Castle echoed. "So, how about you? How was your day?"

"Oh, you know. Just another fun-filled time of chasing bad guys, upholding the law, and keeping the streets safe for the

273

community."

Castle shook his head. "No, really, how did it go?"

"Pretty much like yours. It could have been better."

"The news link on my computer said you're working two cases. Isn't that difficult? I mean, *two* separate murders must be difficult to juggle."

"You actually have time to read the news?"

"When it's of interest to me."

"Sometimes we work more than two. Not often, but it happens. It just depends on the situation. In this instance, though, the two are related."

"Oh. Then that should make it..." He stopped and swallowed.

"Should make it what, Max?"

"I was about to say make it easier. That's an incredibly stupid assumption on my part. A murder case is never easy, is it?"

Before she could answer, the lights on the pager sitting in front of them began to strobe.

"I believe that's our cue," he said.

They located the hostess and were led to a table in the rear of the restaurant.

"Jan, I apologize for assuming your job would be easier." Castle began to peruse the menu. "It's just I've never known a detective before. Or even spoken to one, for that matter. I'm really intrigued by you and what you do."

His honesty and apparent interest in her profession flattered Jan. She had immersed herself in her job to the extent her only social interaction had been with other cops. With the emergence of Crabby Phillips as a friend, a protective insulation from professional burnout was forming around her.

"No apology necessary, Max. In some ways you're right, though. Related cases can sometimes provide more evidence and help us solve them quicker. But every case is different, even though they may appear to be similar or related."

Their server returned and prepared to take their orders. She ordered the seafood gumbo, broiled halibut, and a beer. He selected a dozen oysters, grilled red snapper, and matched her choice of beverage.

"Max, I'm curious why you would come all the way from New Jersey if your business leads weren't solid. It seems like your company is going to a great deal of time and expense by rolling the dice."

Castle gazed at her intently. "Businesses are always looking to stay ahead of the competition. If we, as sales reps, can supply that edge and satisfy their needs, then it's worth the time and effort. The software industry, like any other, is highly competitive. Sometimes the leads you're given are longshots, but if the higher-ups want to risk it, you go where they send you. It's kind of like your profession, but in a different way, of course."

"Well, I hope things turn around quickly before you have to leave."

Castle nodded as he searched the room full of people. "Boy, it's really hard to believe."

"What's hard to believe?"

"I was just thinking out loud. Any one of these people could be a killer." He cut a glance at her. "I suppose that sounds bizarre, doesn't it?"

Jan smiled, but wondered what had initiated such thoughts.

"Don't mind me, Jan. I sometimes watch people and try to figure out who they are, what they do, and where they're going. It's kind of a silly hobby, I guess."

"Not at all, Max, I do the same thing. Only not with everyone. Just with, uh,

persons of interest."

"Okay, I know I shouldn't ask, but how *is* your investigation going?"

Jan sensed another red flag unfurling, but found it difficult to resist him.

"It's getting pretty complicated, but we're considering a

viable theory. Without going into detail, it looks like one person might be going after a specific group of people."

"You mean there are other cases that may be tied to yours?"

She didn't answer.

"You're saying it could be a hitman?"

"I really can't talk about it, Max."

"You're right. I'm doing it again. My curiosity is getting the better of me. It's just I find your line of work so fascinating. And you are, without a doubt, the most interesting woman I have ever met."

Jan's face warmed at his compliment.

Their meals arrived, and the rest of their time together was spent eating and exchanging short, suggestive glimpses.

After dinner, Jan suggested they go to the Sandy Shore Lounge on Pass-a-

Grille Beach for a drink. It was a popular place that played host to a small bar with tables and chairs on the roof. A unique and ideal location for watching the sun setting over the Gulf of Mexico.

Jan led them on the short drive to the lounge, finding plenty of room to park on a side street. Max pulled up behind her. They walked arm in arm to the rear entrance and took the elevator to the roof.

"Oh, good, it's not crowded," Jan said.

"Pick out a table while I get our drinks."

Jan headed for a table in the front corner, the perfect spot to watch the sunset.

Castle returned with their drinks and placed them on the table. Without asking, he removed his sport coat and wrapped it around Jan. "There you go. Feels a bit brisk." He straightened up and looked out over the Gulf. "What a beautiful sight."

"I thought you'd like it here."

The warmth of his coat made warmer the feeling inside Jan, and she was glad she'd decided not to run from the restaurant.

The sun partially immersed in the watery horizon painted a

large bank of clouds to the southwest a dull bronze and held Castle spellbound. "You know, Jan, a few more nights like this and I might never go home."

Jan looked down at her drink, part of her hoping he wouldn't.

They watched the remnants of the sunset fade, the night begin, and the stars proceed to dot the ebony sky.

After a time, Jan glanced at her watch. "Max, I really should be going."

Castle sighed, but didn't object.

They left the lounge and walked to their cars, stopping for a brief and unwanted farewell.

Max looked deeply into Jan's eyes. "I really enjoyed this evening. I hope we can find time for another evening together."

"I'd like that."

He slowly leaned forward to kiss her.

She didn't resist.

CHAPTER 21

The following morning, Jan entered the office humming "Close To You." Jenny was seated at her desk, her hands wrapped around her coffee mug. A dour expression covered her partner's face. "You're late, Sergeant."

"Yes, I am." Jan continued to hum her way to the coffee station.

"I'm glad one of us is happy," Jenny said.

Returning with her coffee, Jan slid into the chair at her desk. "So, what's wrong with you?"

"Ricky didn't call me last night."

Jan shrugged. "Maybe he had an after-hours interview."

"I don't think that's it."

"Is it possible he might be a little nervous because your relationship is going so well?"

"Why would that make him nervous?"

"Maybe he feels he needs some time to think it through. You said he just recently moved here and doesn't have a job. Then he meets you. That's a lot to handle for some people."

Jenny didn't answer.

"Well, what then?"

"I think he's decided he doesn't want to date a cop."

"Don't do this to yourself, Jenny. You don't know what he's thinking."

"St. Pete P.D. interviewed him about the Hobson murder,

didn't they? He's probably pissed off about it and won't ever call me again."

"He did meet with Hobson, Jenny. And, professionally speaking, with him being a suspect, your relationship will have to be put on hold until the case is solved."

"I know. But there may be another reason." Jenny looked down and ran a finger around the rim of her mug. "I figured it was in my best interest to run a search on him."

"A wise decision."

"He told me he was from Drakes Branch, Virginia. It's a small town, and the only Richard Lennon who fits his age and description died six years ago. No one named Rick Lennon owns or is renting a house in Seminole at the address he mentioned to me. It's rental home that belongs to a man named Walter Sinclair who lives in Pensacola.

"Walter Sinclair!"

Jenny's blue eyes went wide. "Oh, my god! Is that Seeward's father? I was so wrapped up in myself it didn't register."

Jan was overwhelmed by a torrent of memories. "I need to call Stan Jeffries." As she picked up her phone, she wondered why this man, whoever he was, would claim to be staying in the house where Seeward was living when he was killed?

CHAPTER 22

Jan put down the receiver. "Jenny, I just told Stan Jeffries what you discovered about Rick. He said they already had that information."

Jenny peered out from the side of her computer monitor. "So when the hell was he going to tell us? I thought you two were going to keep the lines of communication open!"

"He also said James Monroe, the dockmaster at the marina, remembered seeing the Townsend fellow arrive in a dark blue sedan before he left for the day."

Jenny paused. "Ricky drives a dark blue sedan."

"So does Max."

"Do you find it odd we met them at about the same time?"

"I do now."

Jan and Jenny sat in silence and pondered the simultaneous arrival of the two men. Could Rick Lennon and Max Castle be working as a team? Or could an inordinate amount of skepticism be leading the two detectives toward the wrong conclusion? Both men had been moving about the area for the past few days. Both men had equal opportunities to meet with the victims. And worse, both men had recently become friendly with the two of them.

"Is there a chance you might have let something slip while talking to Rick?"

Jan asked. "You know, just in passing?"

Jenny's blue eyes narrowed as she leaned forward. "What the hell is that supposed to mean?"

"Could you have inadvertently discussed our cases with him?"

"No. I would never do that." She studied her partner. "What about you, Sergeant? Is there a chance *you* ran your mouth while visiting with Max?"

"No, I didn't. But Max *has* been awfully curious about what we've been doing. He said he was just interested in my line of work."

Jenny's eyes softened. "Ricky, too. I guess most people are curious about us. But what if it's more than curiosity? What if they're using us?"

A feeling somewhere between helplessness and fury began a measured journey through Jan's mind. Had they been duped? Had they been led into a shadow of deceit by two masterful con artists? Before she could consider the possibility further, the phone on Jenny's desk rang. The one-sided conversation did not sound encouraging.

"What? Aw shit!" Jenny said. "Okay, thanks. Call me the minute you have more information." She slammed down the receiver. "That was my friend with the Tampa P.D.

They just got an anonymous phone call Avery Clendenon has been murdered."

"Damn it!" Jan yelled and pounded her fist on her desk. She sensed the killer or killers they'd been pursuing were about to disappear now all five men on the list had been murdered. "Let's go back to Munyer's condo and go over it again. There has to be something we've overlooked." But she knew it wasn't true. They'd meticulously searched every inch of his condo, although it was better than wallowing in self-pity. At least, that's what she kept telling herself.

CHAPTER 23

Jan arrived home a little after nine o'clock, tired and frustrated. Another search of Murphy Munyer's condo had yielded exactly what she'd expected—nothing. She and Jenny did discover someone had ransacked the unit after their last visit. And that raised another question: what was the intruder searching for? Was it hidden money, jewels, incriminating information, or the missing bank account numbers they found on the disc? The other law enforcement agencies investigating the murders of the business partners hadn't mentioned attempted burglary or vandalism, so why was Munyer targeted?

After she switched on the lights and locked the front door, she laid her phone on the dining table. The headache which began during her ride home was growing stronger as she unbuttoned her blouse. She hadn't slipped out of it when she heard her phone ring.

"Oh, please, not now," she mumbled. "I'm about to collapse."

Picking up her phone, she waited to hear the delivery of more bad news.

"Hi, beautiful, it's Max."

Jan's body tensed, and the pain in her head intensified.

"I stopped by the Spinnaker this evening, hoping to see you." He laughed. "I don't think your friend Crabby likes me very much. I'll be leaving town soon, and I'd like to see you again before I go."

Jan brought a hand to her forehead. "Max, I don't know if I can. It's really getting crazy at work. I'm not sure I'll have the time."

"Oh. I'm sorry. Tell you what, I'll call you right before I leave. Is that okay?"

"Sure."

He wished her well and ended the call.

She cursed herself for having given him her phone number. She'd considered doing a background check when she'd first met him, but it had slipped her mind. First thing in the morning, she would see to it. On her way to the bathroom, her phone rang again. She returned to the dining table and picked up the phone. Caller Unknown, Number Unknown heightened her dismay.

"Sergeant Larkin?"

"Yes."

"This is Don Jennings. I was a close friend of your former partner, Seeward Sinclair."

Chilled by the voice of the man she considered responsible for her partner's death, Jan remembered Jennings and Seeward had communicated during the Janie Ballentine murder case. Though she had no proof, she always suspected he was the supplier of inside information to Seeward as to the whereabouts of Eddie Papalos, and the location of the farmhouse outside Brandon that resulted in both of their deaths.

"Don Jennings? Seeward's friend with the FBI?"

"Look, Sergeant, I feel terrible about what happened to Seeward. But something has come to my attention, and I felt I needed to call you."

"How magnanimous of you. What took you so long?"

"I've become privy to some information which is very important."

"Important, huh? Well, I hope it serves me better than the information you gave Seeward."

"Sergeant, please. Just hear me out."

"I'm listening."

"What I'm about to tell you is highly classified and has to stay between us. If knowledge of this conversation gets out, both of us will be in a lot of trouble."

"I hope it doesn't get both of us killed." She heard Jennings sigh.

"I have a contact with the CIA. Through this contact, I was able to find out Rick Lennon is an alias used by one of their operatives. Lee Overstreet is his name, and he was a childhood friend of Seeward Sinclair. He was a member of a small special operations unit for the CIA that works all over the world. His job was to resolve certain situations without implicating the agency."

"You and Seeward grew up together. Do you know this Overstreet?"

"No, I met Seeward later in high school."

"You said Overstreet *was* a part of the CIA. He's no longer with them?"

"When he learned Seeward had been killed, he ceased all contact with Langley. They haven't been able to find him."

"Hold it right there. They can't find him? With all the technology available today, you want me to believe they can't find one of their own?"

"He's a ghost, Sergeant. A master of disguises. Someone who appears and disappears without leaving a trace. And according to my source, Overstreet was one of the best the agency had."

"And you're telling me this Overstreet is responsible for the two murders we're investigating?"

"He killed all of them."

"What do you mean he killed all of them?"

"There are five men dead who were business partners."

Jan hesitated. Jennings seemed to know as much about the murder cases as she and Jenny. And he'd been right about where Eddie Papalos had been hiding out. "But what do these five men have to do with Seeward's death?"

"There's another partner."

"What's his name?"

"That's all the information I have right now. But there's one last detail you should know, Sergeant. The agency will never admit to the existence of the special ops unit in which Overstreet belonged. In fact, his name might not even be Overstreet. His true identity is known only to a select few inside the agency. In effect, he doesn't exist."

Jan wrote down the phone number where Jennings could be reached before he ended the call. Her headache worsened as she assessed all the information she'd been given. A plan would have to be devised and acted upon soon. And since she'd promised to keep her conversation with Jennings confidential, she couldn't tell Jenny. Switching off the lights, she walked down the short, darkened hall to the bathroom.

CHAPTER 24

Jan hated the idea the Munyer/Parker cases would eventually go cold. The information Don Jennings had given her was the closest thing to a guarantee there was no way to stop it. She looked up from the coroner's report she was reading and noticed Jenny was no longer fixated on her computer monitor. Instead, she was wearing a scowl.

"I have never been this baffled in my entire life," Jenny grumbled. "Even with all the information we've gathered, we still don't have a clue."

"Pun intended?" Jan said.

"That's not funny."

Jan found nothing funny about her weak attempt to lighten the mood either. She'd spent hours in front of the clue board reviewing the evidence and rehashing every theory they could imagine. Even comparing the notes sent them by the detectives working the other cases again. Pride was driving her to prove Don Jennings wrong, but growing doubt reinforced the belief they stood next to no chance of catching Rick Lennon, now known as Lee Overstreet. And she still hadn't told Jenny her acquaintance was a killer. The fact Jenny hadn't spoken of him in days might indicate he was no longer in her life.

"Jenny, you haven't mentioned Rick in a while. Is everything okay?"

"I still haven't heard from him. I don't know what's going

on. I've tried calling him, but he doesn't answer."

"Have you texted him or left a message on his voicemail?"

"Several times. I guess he doesn't have the guts to tell me it's over in person."

Jan felt better at hearing the news, though she knew her partner was unhappy. She felt better because it was becoming clearer to her the man had vanished.

"Larkin, Lester, a word in my office," the lieutenant barked. He turned around and disappeared into the hallway.

Jan shook her head.

"Uh-oh," Jenny said. "Time for another ass chewing." She left her desk and followed Jan to his office.

The lieutenant stood on the left side of his desk, wearing a deeper frown than he'd worn during their last meeting. "Close the door and sit down."

Jan sat down as Jenny closed the door and took a seat in the chair beside her.

"I just finished an hour-long meeting with the sheriff," the lieutenant began. "He wanted a full run-down on the progress of your investigations. I couldn't give him a run-down because, as far as I know, there was nothing new to report. Needless to say, he was less than thrilled. So far, my ass in still intact, but it won't be for long if you don't come up with something soon."

"We're doing the best we can, Lieutenant," Jenny said.

The lieutenant leveled an unsympathetic glare.

Jenny hung her head and shifted in the chair.

He returned his focus to Jan. "Tell me you have a new lead and are close to ending this thing, Sergeant. Tell me something so I can make the sheriff's day."

"Lieutenant, please excuse Detective Lester," Jan said. "We're both on edge because of the lack of progress. This is one of the toughest assignments I've ever worked. All I can tell you is we're continuing to pursue all leads as they surface, and we will put forth the maximum effort to find the killer."

The lieutenant paused for a moment. "Jan, I can't impress

upon you enough the severity of this matter. The other agencies involved are just as eager as we are to close their cases. And from what I hear, they're not having much luck either. By the way, I applaud your cooperating with them. But we've got a serial killer on the loose. The media is having a field day tearing us and the other agencies apart. Do whatever it takes to end this thing. And do it fast." A thin smile creased his lips. "A maximum effort, Sergeant? In what mystery rag did you read that one?"

Jan arched her eyebrows and shrugged.

The Homicide office was alive with activity, but the detectives hardly noticed when they returned to their desks.

"Jan, what are we going to do? We don't have a thing to go on."

"I don't know, Jenny. I don't know."

Jan hated to admit there was nothing more they could do. Unable to stop a killer after he'd left them guessing at every turn was not sitting well with her. And keeping Jenny out of the loop was not only going against her professional beliefs, but breaking her word to never do it again. She avoided total frustration when her phone rang. She sighed and grabbed the receiver.

"Good morning, gorgeous."

"Oh, hi!" A nervous edge lined her voice.

Jenny caught her eye. "Max?" she mouthed.

Jan nodded.

"I promised I would call you again before I left," he said. "Are you feeling better?"

"Yes. And I'm glad you called, but I'm very busy, and I can't talk right now."

"You sound funny. Are you having a rough go of it today?"

"That obvious, huh?"

"Then I'll make this quick. I'm sorry for the late notice, but I'm leaving on Friday. I'd still like to see you before I go. I thought we might catch another sunset tonight. I understand Fort De Soto Park is a good spot. Then, maybe, we could grab a late supper. Somewhere you're comfortable. Does that sound good to you?"

"Yeah, I guess so. How about I meet you at the Spinnaker around six o'clock?"

"I'm looking forward to it."

Jan felt uneasy as she replaced the receiver.

"What's going on?" Jenny asked.

"Max is leaving tomorrow. He wants to get together tonight." She filled Jenny in on the details.

"Is that a good idea? I mean, we're still not sure about him."

Knowing Max Castle wasn't the killer, Jan felt there might be a way to prove his innocence to Jenny. And keep her partner close by until she was certain the real killer was gone. She began to lay out the pieces of her plan. "Max and I will be going to Fort De Soto Park first. I want you to tail us and wait in the parking lot until it's almost dark. Then I want you to find a place to hide that's close enough for you to hear us. As I recall, there are rows of palm trees close to the fort. I'll make sure we don't wind up too close to the water so you can hear us while you're hiding in them."

Jenny nodded.

"I'll keep him talking. Maybe he'll slip up and incriminate himself. If he doesn't,

then follow us to wherever we go to dinner. I'll keep working him. But keep an eye on him at all times. If he catches on to what I'm doing, I'll need your help when it's time to take him."

"Then you should wear a wire, Jan. If I can hear what's going on, then I can get to you faster."

"It's too big a risk."

"Why? You're taking a big risk, anyway."

"Because we'll most likely be hugging and kissing. If he discovers the wire, then he'll know he's being set up."

Jenny sat back, clasped her hands together, and brought them up to her mouth as though she were praying. "Okay, if that's the way you want to do it. But I don't think the lieutenant is going to okay this deal, even if you're wearing a wire. He definitely won't stand for it without having more back-up. And considering this guy may have killed five people, I'm guessing he won't agree to it at all."

Jan stared at her partner.

"What?"

Jan didn't answer.

Jenny wheeled her chair closer. "You're not going to tell him, are you?"

Pushing her chair up to her desk, Jan motioned they should leave with her head.

CHAPTER 25

Jan reached over and gave her friend a gentle shove. "Crabby, stop your complaining. Matt is leaving tomorrow and wants to take me out to eat one last time."

Finishing the last of his beer, Crabby shook his head. "Well, I don't likes it. No, sir. I don't likes it at all. I cain't b'lieve yer gonna see that feller agin. I jus' cain't b'lieve it." He shook his head once more, then looked toward the other end of the bar. "Hank!" he hollered and waved his mug.

"Listen, you lovable old scudder. I'm a big girl and I can take care of myself."

Crabby looked doubtful as set his empty mug on the counter.

"Now what was that for? I'm a cop, Crabby. I've been trained to defend myself."

Hank wiped the counter in front of the old fisherman and set down a full mug.

Crabby picked up the beer. "I know, but yer gonna be out there in the dark with a feller ya don't even know. He might try some funny bidness or sump'um."

He stopped talking when Jan reached over and patted his tanned, wizened hand.

She appreciated his concern. And he was right. She *didn't* know Max Castle. But she knew he wasn't the killer she and Jenny had been chasing. "I'll be okay, Crabby." She patted his hand again.

The two of them felt the presence of the eavesdropper and turned to Hank.

"I agree with Crabby," Hank said.

"I don't r'member nobuddy askin' ya ta spout off 'bout this," Crabby said.

Hank looked at Jan, then back at Crabby. "Okay, okay, I get the message." He latched onto Crabby's empty mug before he left.

"Hello, everybody!" Jenny said. She gave Crabby a playful nudge as she slid into the chair beside him.

"Darlin' Jenny. Am I glad ta see *you*. Mebbe ya can talk some sense inta this knothead 'cause I shore cain't."

"What are you talking about?"

"She's goin' out with that feller agin."

Jenny arched her eyebrows at Jan. "You told him?"

"I *told* him I was going out to eat with Max one last time. Now he's all worried something bad is going to happen."

Jenny leaned into the old salt. "She just wants to see him before he leaves. What's the harm in that?"

Crabby snorted. "Well, I kin see I ain't gonna get no hep from you."

"I guess I'd better go now," Jan said. "I'm supposed to meet Max in a few minutes." Crabby wouldn't look at her, so she bent down and kissed his furry face. "I'll see you tomorrow."

"I'll walk you out," Jenny said.

"Ain't you gonna stay an' keep me comp'ny, darlin'?" Crabby said. "I ain't seen ya in a month o' Sundays, ya know."

"I can't. I have to run some errands and...do my laundry."

"Then why'd ya come by?"

Jenny shrugged. "Habit, I guess. I'll stop by tomorrow. We'll talk then. I promise."

Jan sighed when she and Jenny reached the front door. "I really hate having to lie to Crabby."

"Don't worry, Jan. He'll be all right."

Jan looked over her shoulder at him. Crabby was staring into his beer mug.

CHAPTER 26

Jan leaned against her car and struggled with her conscience while waiting for Max. She had deceived Jenny by not breaking her word to Don Jennings, lied to Crabby about her reason for wanting to see Max, and now she was going to lie again.

Castle arrived at exactly six o'clock and greeted Jan with a lingering kiss and lengthy hug. "I'm really glad you could make it."

"I'm looking forward to it."

"What's the quickest way to get to the fort? I don't want to miss one minute of *this* sunset."

Jan offered her best smile as he opened the door to the dark blue sedan. She would have to put on a convincing act.

Once they had pulled onto Gulf Boulevard, she instinctively looked over her shoulder. Through the rear window, she saw Jenny's car waiting to leave the parking lot.

"Are we being followed?" Castle said and laughed.

Jan's stomach tightened. "Force of habit." Satisfied the plan was in motion, she gave Castle's shoulder a squeeze and turned around.

Castle talked away the miles as they left Treasure Island via the Blind Pass Bridge and rolled into St. Petersburg Beach on Blind Pass Road. At 75th Avenue, they turned right for a short stretch until another turn put them back onto Gulf Boulevard.

Castle sang the community's praises as he scanned the

surroundings. "I can't get over this. So many lounges and bars. It seems like there's one on every corner. And the souvenir shops. How do they stay in business when they all advertise the same merchandise?" He laughed. "And look at the little motels between those gigantic condominiums and hotels. If it wasn't for them, you couldn't see the water."

Jan nodded, smiled, and sometimes offered a brief opinion in an effort to keep him preoccupied. As he rambled on, she was thinking about how to keep him between the shoreline and the row of palm trees where Jenny would be hiding as they watched the sunset. She would engage in light conversation like on their first date and not ask too many questions.

Approaching Bayway Road, the only passage leading to Tierra Verde from Gulf Boulevard, she directed him into the left turn lane.

Castle did as she instructed, then jerked his head to the right. "Holy guacamole! What is that?"

"That's the Don Cesar Beach Resort."

"It looks like a castle. No pun intended."

Jan laughed. "It was built in 1928, and hosted people like F. Scott Fitzgerald, Clarence Darrow, and Al Capone. They used to call it The Pink Palace. The Veteran's Administration moved in for a while, but later it was abandoned. In 1973, it was reclaimed as a hotel and then renovated in 1994."

"Well, aren't you the walking history book. I'm impressed. You should be a tour guide in your spare time."

"What spare time?"

Castle laughed. After feeding the toll booth before they drove onto the bridge, he was again taken in by another sight. "Houses sitting right on the water? Is that an island?"

"That's Vina del Mar. There's a bridge leading to it a little farther down Gulf Boulevard."

"Imagine that. Fishing from your own backyard. My associates back home are not going to believe me when I tell them."

Castle's manner and style were convincing, maybe even

honest, but Jan knew better than to allow her emotions to take control. He was leaving tomorrow. She figured she would never see him again. It was good he was enchanted by the sights. Keeping his mind occupied kept his eyes away from the rearview mirror and the chance of spotting Jenny. She directed him to the turn for the Pinellas Bayway. They sailed along the two-lane stretch of road until they crossed another bridge.

"Max, this is Tierra Verde," Jan said. "In the sixties, Guy Lombardo had a resort here named Port O' Call."

"Really?"

"Quite a few big-name acts played the nightclub."

"And here I thought St. Petersburg was just a place where people came to retire."

Another long, flat stretch of road divided by a median laid before them.

Castle was rubbernecking again and became distracted when he saw the many mansions fronted by Mud Bayou. "Would you look at that! I'll bet royalty lives there."

"That's Millionaire's Island, and the name pretty much says it all."

A few miles later, the asphalt corridor led them over another bridge to Mullet Key. At the next intersection of Anderson Boulevard, they turned right and headed west toward their final destination, Fort De Soto.

Castle let go with a heavy sigh. "Look at all this wilderness. Even with all the condominiums we saw on the way, it's easy to understand why so many people want to come here."

Jan was well aware what he'd said was true. Mullet Key and several small islands comprised the county park. Other than a few pavilions and buildings, the acreage was virtually untouched, and had been since the time when a boat was needed to explore the tropical paradise. Minutes later, they pulled into the parking lot on the southern end of the fort.

"Let's go down to the water, Jan," Castle said.

Jan let go with nervous laughter as she opened the door.

Swinging her legs to the asphalt, she patted her pants leg to make certain her backup revolver was still secure in her ankle holster. They began their hike through the sand, wandering closer to the water's edge than she would have preferred. Castle stopped walking and took hold of her hand. She fought the urge to glance over her shoulder. Half of a red-orange sun sat atop the Gulf of Mexico. The surrounding sky shone pastel yellows, greens, and blues, the glowing water an electric turquoise. Above the sun, a cluster of rust-tinged clouds drifted north. A pair of seagulls glided overhead, letting loose with a chorus of squawks. A light, salt-tinged breeze that enveloped them highlighted the moment.

"I don't think I could ever get tired of this," Castle said.

Twilight then nightfall finally overcame the sun and allowed a countless number of stars to twinkle brightly over the darkened expanse. Castle squeezed Jan's hand and faced her. "I didn't want to leave without telling you how glad I am we met. And that I…"

"That you what?" she whispered.

He raised his hands and cupped her shoulders. "That I've fallen in love with you,

Jan. I know that sounds crazy. We don't even know each other. But I felt I just had to tell you."

Jan struggled to avoid surrendering to his claim, her self-defense beginning to crumble. Castle leaned forward to kiss her.

"Now, isn't that sweet?" said a voice from behind them.

They both jumped and spun around. A man stood silhouetted against the stark glow of the parking lot lights. Jan couldn't see his face clearly. The only recognizable feature was his blonde hair glowing as white as the sand beneath her feet. "Who are you? What do you want?"

"We've never met, Jan, but your partner knows me."

Jan hesitated. "You're Rick Lennon, aren't you?"

"Jenny said you were the best detective she'd ever seen." Lennon raised the silenced automatic from his left side and pointed it at Castle. "Now tell her who *you* really are, Johnny."

"Johnny?" Jan said.

"Don't listen to him, Jan!" Castle shouted. "He's the one you're after."

"Now, how would he know anything about your investigation, Jan? You didn't tell him, did you?"

"No," Jan said.

"Jenny never said a word to me, so how would he know?"

Jan didn't answer.

"Does the name Papalos mean anything to you? Of course it does. Your friend here is Johnny Papalos, Eddie's brother."

"He's lying, Jan!"

"Johnny's been playing you to get to me. His boss is Colby Rittenhouse."

Fury raced through Jan as she glared at the man who'd deceived her. The gambit was now perfectly clear. She and Jenny had been pawns in a deadly game of search and destroy by two men bent on killing each other. She started toward Lennon. "Why you son of a—"

Lennon shifted his automatic. "Don't do that, Jan. I'm not here for you."

"So, I'm supposed to let you kill him and just walk away? Is that it?"

"It's best if you do. I don't want to hurt you, Jan, but if you press me, I'll have no other choice." Lennon raised his automatic higher.

Papalos grabbed Jan and threw her at Lennon. The high-pitched report from the silenced automatic pierced the air, and a bullet tore into her shoulder. Jan screamed and collapsed as Papalos reached inside his jacket. Lennon shoved Jan to the ground and wheeled his pistol in time to pump two rounds into the chest of the Rittenhouse soldier. Papalos staggered backward, then slumped into the shallows. Lennon searched every direction before approaching Papalos. He paused a moment to watch one wave after another decorate the man's lifeless body with foam. Then he kicked him in the ribs. Papalos didn't move. Satisfied his quarry was dead, Lennon bent down, relieved the gunsel of his automatic, and flung it into the water.

Jan lay motionless on her back as a dark stain spread across the right shoulder of her blouse. Lennon knelt down beside her. He placed two fingers on the side of her neck and felt for a pulse. She moaned before opening her eyes.

"I'm sorry, Jan. I'm sorry about Jenny, too. But I had to do it, all of it, for Seeward." He stood up and looked around one last time then vanished into the darkness.

"Not Jenny," Jan whispered. "Not again." She groaned and was about to lose consciousness when she heard a voice call out in the distance.

Jenny came running up. Shock covered her face when she saw Jan lying on the ground. "Oh, god, no!" She yanked her phone from the pocket of her slacks and punched 911. "This Detective Jennifer Lester, Pinellas County Sheriff's Office. I've got an officer down behind Fort De Soto. I need an ambulance now." She dropped to her knees. "Jan? Jan, can you hear me?"

"I hear you," Jan said. Then she passed out.

CHAPTER 27

An irritating beeping sounded in measured intervals, interrupting the lovely spring morning in the country Jan was sharing with her father. The dream faded, and she caught the sterile odor of antiseptic as she slowly opened her eyes. "Someone shut that damned thing off," she mumbled. Confused by the sight of a blurry light green wall, she started to sit up. A stabbing pain in her right shoulder forced her to fall back into the hospital bed.

"Don't move, Jan," Jenny said. "Just stay still."

Jan still couldn't focus, but was able to make out the three fuzzy figures standing beside her bed.

"Just relax, Detective." The male voice was unfamiliar. "You're in the hospital and you're going to be fine."

As her eyes cleared, Jan discovered Jenny, Crabby, and a stranger in a long white coat peering down at her.

"We had a difficult time removing that bullet, so we're going to keep you here awhile as a precautionary measure. I'm Doctor Ted Beecher. I'll be checking on you from time to time."

"Crabby," Jan croaked.

The old salt clasped her right hand and gave it a gentle squeeze. "Don't ya worry none, Jan. I ain't goin' nowhere."

"Jenny...are you all right?"

"I'm fine," Jenny said.

Jan saw a deep purple lump on her partner's forehead. "I

remember Overstreet saying he was sorry for what he'd done to you. I thought he'd shot you, too."

Jenny rubbed the sizeable bump. "It was Rick, Jan. He snuck up behind me while I was in the trees watching you and Max. When I asked him what he was doing there, the son of a bitch clobbered me. Who is Overstreet?"

"I want Detective Larkin to get some rest now, so everyone out," Beecher said.

"No, Doctor, please," Jan said. "I have something important to tell them."

"You can tell them tomorrow."

"Doctor, ten minutes is all I need. Please."

Beecher glanced at Jenny and Crabby. "Ten minutes, but not a second longer."

Jan waited until he was gone. "Jenny, Crabby, I lied to both of you. And I'm sorry. I got a call from Don Jennings. He told me about Rick Lennon." She looked at Crabby. "Jennings works for the FBI and was a friend of Seeward's."

Crabby nodded.

"Jenny, he made me promise not to tell you Rick Lennon was really a CIA operative named Lee Overstreet. He was also a friend of Seeward's. Jennings told me when Overstreet found out Seeward had been killed, he left the agency. Just disappeared. They had no idea of where he had gone."

"But, Jan," Crabby said, "how coulda feller jus' up an' disappear?"

"It was a part of his job, Crabby. He used disguises when he was assigned to remedy problems all over the world. And according to Jennings, he was a ghost."

"A ghost? Ya mean like he weren't really alive?"

"I'll explain it to you later," Jenny said. "So, Rick was the one doing all the killings?"

"Yes, Jenny," Jan said, "and I'm sorry, but it appears he was using you to make certain we and the other agencies weren't closing in on him."

"But I didn't tell him anything."

"He may have been watching you without you knowing it. He may have been watching all of us."

Crabby's mouth dropped open.

"He was that good at disguising himself?" Jenny said.

"One of the best, according to Jennings."

Jenny lowered her eyes, then looked up. "So, why were we following Max Castle?"

"That's where I lied to you. Until I heard from Don Jennings, Max was still a suspect. I knew he wasn't the one we were after, but when you said you hadn't heard from Rick, I figured he'd vanished. Having you tail Max was to prove he wasn't the killer. I'm sorry, Jenny."

"And that's why you suggested we not tell the lieutenant what we were planning to do."

"Sure. What's the worst that could happen?"

"I guess we found out. But now I'm really confused. If Max wasn't the one we were after, then why the hell did Rick knock me out?"

Jan sighed. "This is where my lying to you worked out for the best. Max Castle was really Johnny Papalos, Eddie Papalos's brother."

"No way."

"Who's this 'ere Pappy-los?" Crabby said.

"Eddie Papalos killed Seeward," Jan said. "Rick told me Max was sent by Colby Rittenhouse to kill him for murdering his five business partners."

"There's that name again," Jenny said. "Damn that Rittenhouse anyway."

"I hear that. Let's hope we're rid of him forever."

"Speaking of the business partners, do you think it was Rick who rummaged through Murphy Munyer's condo looking for their offshore bank account information?"

"Rick or, possibly, Max. He was hoping to use me to get to Rick, and may also have been ordered to find the account numbers. I guess we'll never know for sure. But considering the way everything turned out, I sure am glad you had my back, Jenny."

"Me, too," Crabby said.

"Well, that's it," Jenny said. "No more men for me. I'm tired of being used and then tossed aside. From now on I'm going to enjoy the single life." She noticed Crabby staring at her. "All right. I'll make room for you." She leaned over and kissed him.

Crabby pulled away and wiped off his face. "Now stop that!"

Jan laughed. "Ow!" She grasped her shoulder. "I shouldn't have done that."

"Do it hurt bad?"

"Only when my friends make me laugh."

"We'd better go," Jenny said. "Crabby's going to take me out in his boat soon."

"Would you mind waiting until I get out of here so I can join you?" Jan said. "My shoulder bone wasn't broken, and depending on my progress, I should be out of here in a week or so."

Jenny looked at Crabby. "I think we can do that."

"Thanks again, Jenny. You saved my life."

Jenny smiled.

"You two are the best people I know," Jan said.

Crabby looked away and laid a hand below his brow.

"What's wrong, Crabby? You're not crying, are you?"

"No, I jus'…got sump'um in muh eye."

She looked at Jenny.

"Me, too," Jenny said and smiled.

Jan watched a small tear escape down her partner's cheek.

CHAPTER 28

Jan focused on the horizon separating the mid-morning blue sky and the blue-green water, the last few weeks still vivid in her mind. Her brush with death exposed a vulnerability she'd never known before. The end could come at any time. Best to appreciate every moment of every day. And the time with those you love.

A breeze brushed her face, and its salty smell brought her thoughts back to the chugging engines of the trawler and her friends nearby. Crabby, at the wheel, guiding them further into the Gulf. Jenny, on his right, whose friendship she coveted.

Jan sighed as the sound of the cars passing over the John's Pass bridge behind them faded to the rhythmic slapping of the waves against the hull. "Jenny, we need to do this more often. It's always so peaceful out here."

"You won't get an argument from me," Jenny said. She nudged Crabby. "You have any objections?"

"I spent most o' muh life on the sea, darlin'. Best place I knows ta cure what ails ya."

Jan wrapped her arm around his waist as Jenny laid her head on his shoulder. She knew the bond between them would never be broken.

ACKNOWLEDGMENTS

Thanks to George Salter, Claire Kemp, Theresa R. Richardson, D.T. Bush, Sue Lloyd-Davies, Patricia Grayson, Heloise Jones, Tom Horrigan, Joyce Wagner, the Gulfport Fiction Writers, David Mather and the Gulfport Public Library, Technical Advisors Rod Steckel and Ken Beaudoin, Alex Cameron, Dia and the wonderful folks at the Neptune Bar and Grill, and Gini and Mike of the Beach Bazaar. Special thanks to Lynn Taylor, Steph Post, Jeffery Hess, and Johnnie M. Clark for their guidance, support, and friendship. Many thanks to my dear friends Mike O'Malley, John and Nancy Lamson, Al and Nancy Karnavicius, Rim Karnavicius and Michelle Rego, Charles Lyon, and Jim and Debby Herden. And most of all, I wish to express my grateful appreciation for my family.

Photo credit Sue Lloyd-Davies

STEPHEN BURDICK was born and raised in Florida. He is a retired civil servant currently living in the Tampa Bay area. He enjoys getting together with friends and attending various events.

DOWN & OUT BOOKS

On the following pages are a few
more great titles from the
Down & Out Books publishing family.

For a complete list of books and to
sign up for our newsletter,
go to DownAndOutBooks.com.

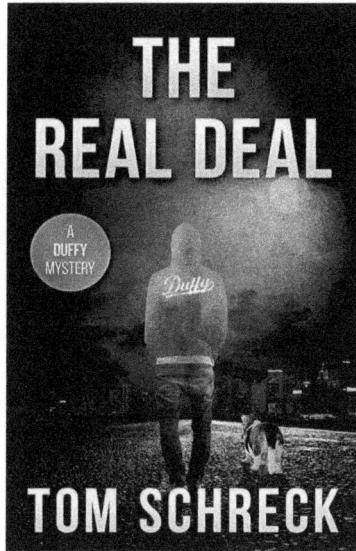

The Real Deal
A Duffy Mystery, 7th in Series
Tom Schreck

Down & Out Books
November 2023
978-1-64396-361-7

When Mushie, the popular street hustler of counterfeit watches, sneakers, and kitchen gadgets, comes into Duffy's bar bleeding from a gunshot wound to the stomach, Duffy and the gang are baffled. Everyone loved Mush who didn't have a mean bone in his body, Sure, he operated on the edges of what's considered proper society but, hey, so did a lot of Duffy's friends.

For Duffy, it's different. Mush was Hymie's, Duff's father-like mentor, grandson, and Duff had promised to keep an eye out for him. Now, it meant righting Mushie's wrong after his death.

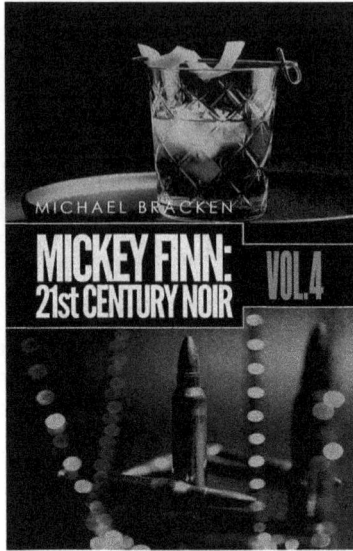

Mickey Finn: 21st Century Noir Vol. 4
Michael Bracken, Editor

Down & Out Books
December 2023
978-1-64396-346-4

Mickey Finn: 21st Century Noir, Volume 4, the fourth volume of the hard-hitting series, is another crime-fiction cocktail that will knock readers into a literary stupor.

Contributors push hard against the boundaries of crime fiction, driving their work into places short crime fiction doesn't often go, into a world where the mean streets seem gentrified by comparison and happy endings are the exception, not the rule.

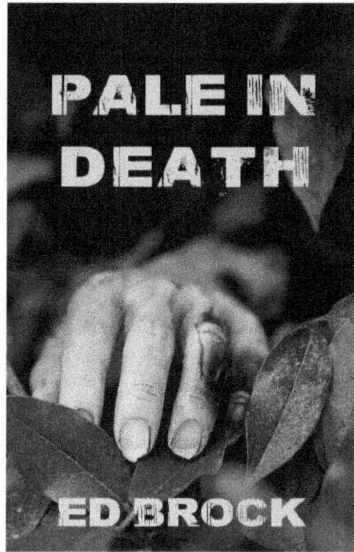

Pale in Death
Ed Brock

Down & Out Books
January 2024
978-1-64396-351-8

Reporter Mark Freer learns that the body of an old girlfriend has been found, beaten to death, in the county where he now lives and works south of Atlanta. He left the girl, Amanda, years before due to her drug addiction but feels guilty because he played a part in beginning that addiction.

Driven by that guilt, he begins to investigate Amanda's death.

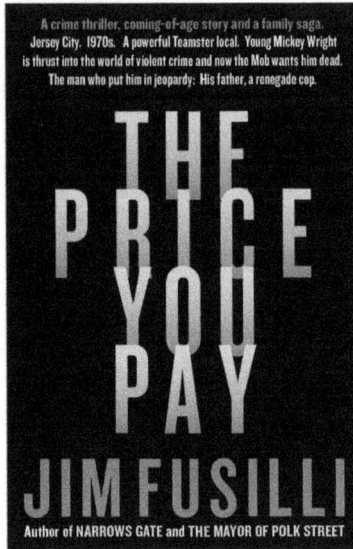

A crime thriller, coming-of-age story and a family saga.
Jersey City. 1970s. A powerful Teamster local. Young Mickey Wright
is thrust into the world of violent crime and now the Mob wants him dead.
The man who put him in jeopardy: His father, a renegade cop.

THE PRICE YOU PAY

JIM FUSILLI

Author of NARROWS GATE and THE MAYOR OF POLK STREET

The Price You Pay
Jim Fusilli

Down & Out Books
January 2024
978-1-64396-352-5

A crime thriller and coming-of-age story, *The Price You Pay*
unravels in crumbling Jersey City where violence and coercion
reign.

Young Mickey Wright is thrust by his father, a free-wheeling
policeman well-known to politicians and drug dealers, into a
world controlled by a powerful Teamster local associated with
the Genovese crime syndicate.

www.ingramcontent.com/pod-product-compliance
Lightning Source LLC
Chambersburg PA
CBHW031140020426
42333CB00013B/460